what others are saying...

"Endlessly curious, opinionated and knowledgeable on the essentials of attracting customers, Martha and Chris are clear-eyed about what coaches need to do to build their business."
—KAREN KIMSEY-HOUSE, CEO, Coaches Training Institute

"If your product, service or issue isn't catching on, Martha Hanlon and Chris Williams will show you how to change that and fast and affordably."
—JOHN LIMBOCKER, Internet Dominator CEO and Godfather of SEO

"Just two of Hanlon's and Williams' strategies completely changed my business. They enabled me to reach so many more people and to turn those contacts into sales. Not only that my new customers are referring their friends, sending testimonials and sharing in their networks. I had been working so hard on my own, but with their help and genius I now have a staff of people working with me. Their advice worked even better than I had thought it would."
—REVEREND JENNIFER HADLEY, Minister, spiritual teacher, counselor and creator of Living a Course in Miracles

"This book is dynamite! Hanlon and Williams blast through the mysteries of marketing hype to deliver what entrepreneurs need most: A savvy, accessible guide to connecting with your target audience and attracting the customers your business deserves."

—KAREN HAGER, Out of the Fog LLC

"As the world moves faster and faster towards sameness, every business has to figure out how to stand out or get drowned out. Hanlon has always taken a simple yet innovative approach that enables businesses at all stages to find what is compelling and breakthrough about them so they're able to own their brand's voice in the market."

—PROMISE PHELON, CEO, Upwardly Mobile

"For any business seeking to earn more clients, *Customers Are The Answer to Everything* offers surprising yet practical insights. Hanlon and Williams provide an approach that flat-out works no matter what size your business is or aspires to be."

—BRONWYN ROSE, Director, CornerPiece

"I've had the privilege of working alongside many great marketing minds, but Martha and Chris stand out with their unique talent that makes marketing understandable, do-able --and even fun!-- for any small business or entrepreneur."

—SUSAN RAAB, Content Wheel

"For all you harried entrepreneurs out there—and is there any other kind—*Customers Are the Answer to Everything* shows you precisely how to prosper by finding and engaging the most important asset any business can have."

—JIM AND LORRAINE CONAWAY, Founders, Conaway & Conaway Financial Strategists

"As a Solo-preneur, I'm the marketing and sales department. Martha and Chris understand the resources a small business owner has to work with, and they showed me exactly how to get the most out of me, my time and limited budget."
— **LISA PAVIN**, President, Bridge to Retirement

"I feel more comfortable speaking about my business to others. This is because Martha & Chris helped me develop an understanding of what I offer. The words come to mind easier. I focus on networking rather than sales and what I offer gets worked in naturally."
— **BEV NOWAKOWSKI**, Friend With A Camera

"Martha and Chris explain marketing in a straight forward, easy to understand way without a lot of buzz words and technical jargon. They take you step by step through finding out what your core business is, identifying who your ideal customer is and where you find them. They then continued on with building a marketing plan, a 24 month plan for your business, how you can reach your customers and followed it up with homework EVERY week plus hold you accountable for the homework! We are treating 'Sales and Marketing' a little differently these days."
— **CAPTAIN DOUG and GALA REITZ**, Sterling Travel Group

"It simply has been the most productive, well-organized, and rich experience as compared to, probably too many others, that I have paid handsomely for with far fewer results. The energy between the two of you is contagious and offers much integrity. Clearly, your techniques are tried and true and your efforts to stay informed evident. Bottom line, you both are so humble, approachable and downright likeable! I remain in deep gratitude."
— **MARY HOBRATSCHK**, Life At Hand

"Martha & Chris have been invaluable mentors to me in the area of marketing. They have identified strategies and actions that will work in my business. They are extremely talented and great to work with as well as having a strong commitment to quality and very customer focused. I am very appreciative that I have someone of their expertise to turn to for advice. They are very passionate about their work in Marketing and I can tell they really enjoy finding success for their clients. They are very generous with their information so their ideas and thoughts have definitely been a benefit to me."

—MONICA BREWER, Director, SHE Business

"Creating my vision of where I want to be in 24 months was eye opening. Making it so clear that there are no questions unanswered has changed my way of thinking. Bringing that even closer to the 12 month period makes it even more real to me. This brings everything into focus for me."

—JUDY HOBERMAN, Selling In A Skirt

"The first time I heard Martha speak, I knew that she knew more about 'marketing' in her little finger than all of the other experts I had ever heard, combined! And, I was right. Then, she and her partner, Chris Williams, changed my business based on what was in their little fingers. Now they'll change every business that buys this book and does what they tell you to do."

—PHIL NEAL WALKER, CEO, Phil Neal Walker Law Corporation, speaker and author

"There are two new superstars on the marketing horizon, Martha Hanlon and Chris Williams. We have two new names on the marketing horizon who have the talent and insight to stand beside the greatest marketers of our time."

—JILL LUBLIN, Master PR Strategist, international speaker and author of three best-selling books including *Get Noticed, Get Referrals*

"These are the very marketing and sales strategies that our business is using to attract new clients. The strategies are created with the budgets of small business owners in mind, and most cost little-to-nothing to implement."

—PETER IVETT, Director, Vivente

CUSTOMERS ARE THE ANSWER to EVERYTHING

How to Get and **KEEP** All the Customers Your Business Wants

MARTHA HANLON & CHRIS WILLIAMS

MORGAN JAMES PUBLISHING • NEW YORK

CUSTOMERS ARE THE ANSWER to EVERYTHING

ISBN: 978-1-61448-107-2 (Paperback)
   978-1-61448-108-9 (eBook)
Library of Congress Control Number: 2011935922P

Published by:
MORGAN JAMES PUBLISHING
1225 Franklin Ave Ste 32
Garden City, NY 11530-1693
Toll Free 800-485-4943
www.MorganJamesPublishing.com

Cover/Interior Design by:
Rachel Lopez
rachel@r2cdesign.com

For our best parts,
Judy and Ty,
400 dogs and 900 kids,
and every client and customer we've worked with
over the past decade.

table of contents

———————————————————————— PART THREE: EXPANSION

foreword

S ometimes books just have to be written... and read. Those were my thoughts when I first examined the initial chapters of *Customers Are The Answer to Everything*.

The wonderful book you hold in your hands delivers a clear, concise and unique system for bringing customers into your business. You'll reconstruct your business marketing and sales, but more important, you'll adjust your relationship with your prospects and customers. Martha Hanlon and Chris Williams have honed their knowledge, belief and years of results into an amazing method to guide you to attract the customers you want... and keep them.

Many authors have written about marketing—including myself. As an expert in easy and inexpensive strategies for small business, I recognize that marketing is not a natural skill for most entrepreneurs and small business owners. Yet each owner must step up to the task or face the possible extinction of their business. *Customers Are The Answer to Everything* shows you how to conquer the struggles and conflicts that marketing represents in your psyche, relationships and, most of all, efforts.

Martha and Chris have wisdom—and it shows through. Their dedication to the achievement of their own customers is obvious as is their desire for your success.

Like my book, *Guerrilla Marketing*, this book is about concepts, a system and action. Don't just read it. Go do what they tell you.

—JAY CONRAD LEVINSON
The Father of Guerrilla Marketing
Entrepreneur

the year
of the customer

Everywhere you turn, the media message is clear: entrepreneurs are the secret to U.S. economic success. Small business will drive the rise of the economic health of the nation.

We're sure that's true. If you look at Fortune 500 companies, their year-to-year growth generally hovers in the single digits. Boosting their value on Wall Street takes more than single digits. So they go out and buy double-digit, high growth small businesses, start-ups and medium-sized companies to enhance their perceived market value.

But here's the question no one seems to be asking: if entrepreneur-driven, small businesses boost the economy, what boosts the entrepreneur?

We ask that question every day. Here's the answer.

Customers. Lots and lots of customers.

Forget the talk about this being the Year of the Entrepreneur. It's really The Year of the Customer.

Which brings us to you.

How is your business doing? Do you have enough customers? Do you engage and serve them? Do you know precisely where to go to find your Ideal Prospect?

If not, this book intends to show you how to attract all the customers you want so you can celebrate The Year of the Customer...and The Year of You, the Entrepreneur.

Attracting your Ideal Prospect is the job of marketing. Then sales takes over to turn them into customers. And how we need to market has changed substantially. The economy, constant new Internet technologies, and changes in what drive your Ideal Prospects to act—or not act—mean that whatever you learned about marketing years ago probably doesn't work anymore.

Yet as the CEO of your business, or head of marketing or sales, you need to understand all these changes and market in the new ways that your customer requires, technologies enable and the economy demands.

Let's face it. When you started your business it probably wasn't because you loved marketing. You went into business because you loved being a coach, a chiropractor, a chocolate maker, a CPA, attorney or whatever it is that you do.

You had visions of a constant stream of customers who appreciated you and eagerly referred others. The demand for your services would keep expanding and you would have the freedom to joyfully do what it is that you love to do—all the way to the bank.

BECOMING A MARKETING AND SALES WIZARD WAS NOT PART OF YOUR DREAM.

Maybe you even "hate" marketing. You've likely already spent a lot of money trying to figure it out, hire it out, or make it go away. And it hasn't worked or at least not like you want it to.

Perhaps you've convinced yourself that you're just missing the marketing gene, that you're just not good at it. Perhaps the whole world of marketing, Internet strategies and social networking overwhelms and gives you such a gigantic headache that you find yourself day-dreaming about taking a job as a barista, happily spending your days steaming milk for lattes.

Well, put down that milk and back away from the counter. Step up to embracing your business and decoding what really will work for your business—and for your Ideal Prospect.

AN EXPERT BY YOUR SIDE

We feel your pain because we've been there. We've got big marketing educations, worked for some of the finest companies in America, started many businesses of our own and made our share of mistakes. We now have PhDs in entrepreneurial street smarts.

Along the way, we've discovered how to market effectively and come up with just the right customer for you. Finding one who's eager to be your Forever Customer isn't so hard. It's just no one's made it simple.

You are about to demystify the marketing process because through this book, we're going to break it down into specific action steps for you. Then you'll have the answers that will turn things around in your business, so that you become someone who "gets" marketing. And we want you to be great at it.

Despite what you might think, marketing is really not that complicated. Like anything new that you embark on, there's always that feeling that something's missing, something that you must not be "getting."

We know this feeling you have. We've worked with, trained and coached thousands of business

THE SECRET TO A THRIVING BUSINESS LIES IN GENERATING CUSTOMERS.

builders just like you. We've helped our customers generate over a million new leads and $64 million in revenue in the last four years.

We want to change the way you think about marketing. More importantly, we want to change the way you attract new customers. Where would your business be—where would any business be—without customers?

Let's go get you some. All you want. All you deserve.

IT'S ALL ABOUT THE CUSTOMER

Customer Generator System

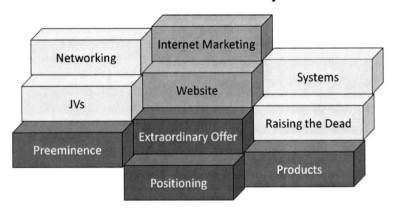

You're holding the blueprint for success in your hands right now. **The Customer Generator System**™ shows you the steps you need to take to get more customers. And unlike many complicated systems out there, Customer Generator System is built on three concepts:

- Foundation
- Activation
- Expansion

First, you will build a strong **Foundation**. Without a solid foundation you can spend a lot of money, invest tons of your precious time, be extremely busy but not accomplish what you targeted. It's a lot like building a house. Build a strong foundation so you won't be banging away on something that will eventually fall apart.

With your Foundation in place, you're ready to put the **Activation** steps in motion. These actions are targeted at dramatically increasing the number of customers you attract to your business—and that means more revenue, which translates into a very happy you.

Finally, **Expansion** hands you the systems and support to keep building your business momentum.

With these three pieces in place, never again will you waste energy worrying about how to get more customers. Instead, you'll focus on how to serve them even more fabulously.

You'll find lots of worksheets and thought-inducing forms throughout this book. They are all downloadable—for FREE—at www. wideawakemarketing.com/resources. Go grab them now so you can build your own blueprint and track your execution as you work through each chapter.

PART ONE

The Foundation

Want people to "get" what you do? First you've got to "get it" yourself, and probably in a different way than you have before. Don't waste any more time and money chasing customers until you master the tools that help you catch and keep them.

Preeminence
KNOW THY CUSTOMERS AND LEAD THEM

Leadership. *Every great business follows a powerful leader. You need to be that leader in your business.*

Vayu Rasta Institute trained more yoga instructors than any company on the planet. Following their unique training system, their students integrated their method and had fun in the process. Yet in their humility, Vayu Rasta never shared this leadership with their market. Wouldn't you want to know when you're working with the best?

Many small businesses are just like Vayu Rasta Institute. They fail to share what makes them uniquely qualified, what makes them an expert.

The first step in establishing a strong foundation for your business is for you to stand in your power, the center of your knowledge and skill that makes you an expert. This is the principle of "Preeminence." Preeminence means "to stand out; to have paramount rank or superiority; to have dignity and importance." This is what one our mentors, Jay Abraham,

TO BE WILDLY SUCCESSFUL YOU MUST KNOW AND LEAD YOUR CUSTOMER.

teaches. To be "Preeminent" in your business, you will balance two critical factors: knowing your customer and leading them.

You must know and empathize with your customers to understand their need, their problem, and their desire. You must know them to understand the shoes they walk in and what they want to accomplish.

You must lead them because, frankly, you know more about your subject than they do. Without arrogance or boastfulness, you must take your customer where they want to go—because you've been there millions of times before and know the way.

DO YOU REALLY *KNOW* WHAT YOUR CUSTOMER WANTS?

Too many small business owners forget they need to know their customer. They think they only need to know the product or service they offer. They forget their Ideal Prospect doesn't know everything that they, as the experts, know.

We've all been to a doctor who started spouting off what was wrong with you, even though you had no idea what she was talking about. You might have gone to her office believing you had a certain ailment. Suddenly, she's talking about something else—if only you could understand what the heck she was saying. She tells you what's ailing you in the language of a doctor, but you're not a doctor, are you? You don't have her language or her knowledge of the human body. And there she is talking to you like you had just completed your Fellowship in Internal Medicine.

If that doctor really understood her patients, she would speak to them in English. Many business owners make the same mistake. They start yakking. Instead, *listen*. And ask. Ask key questions that gather useful information. Then speak in the language your customer understands.

THE SECRET TO ENGAGING CUSTOMERS LIES IN ASKING THEM WHAT THEY WANT.

Too many business people—in small, medium and large businesses—sit isolated in their office dreaming up some ideas that they think "for sure" their customers will want. They know because, well, because they just do. They fall hopelessly in love with their business and ideas. They launch with a big "Ta Dah!" But instead of cheers, they are greeted by the sounds of crickets.

Ginny, one of our customers, is a great example. Ginny operated in isolation when she first launched her business. She finally saw the light—with our push—and decided it was time to learn what was going on with her customer.

She interviewed 50 potential Ideal Prospects and current customers. What she discovered she thought they needed, they didn't connect with. She uncovered the problem as *they saw it*, not as Ginny The Expert knew it. Now she had the information she needed to talk to them in their language about how they perceived their needs.

Ginny learned a valuable lesson. No one can get a Prospect to buy something they don't think they need.

Once Ginny understood what their problem was, she could connect them to her solution…for that problem. Ginny now understood how to lead her customers to their right solution and to her expertise. Now she's found new life in her business coupling the needs of her customer together with her Preeminence, her expertise, through her Leadership.

A "thinking" entrepreneur might decide that a little marketing will move their beautiful, new product into the hands of hundreds, even thousands of customers. But if the product doesn't solve the customer's problem *as they perceive it*, no marketing program can be fabulous enough to get them to buy it—at least not enough of them. You'll be busy trying to sell them the answer to a problem they don't think they have. That's a non-starter.

Then there's the "make money" business owner. He typically becomes so focused on profits he doesn't see the customer. He prioritizes money over everything else, either because he is greedy or panicked at not having enough to make a living. He's mistaken the proverbial golden egg for the goose.

What's the solution? Fall in love with your customer instead.

FALL IN LOVE WITH YOUR CUSTOMER

When you fall in love with your customer and you give them what they require, you will succeed. It's fool proof. It works every time. Not just some of the time, *all of the time.* You'll have customers eager to work with you—so many you won't know what to do with them. (And doesn't that sound like a happy problem?)

There is a little trick—you knew there would be.

Your customers don't always know what they want.

Twenty years ago, if some foresighted interviewer had asked whether you'd like to buy the Internet, you would have said "NO. And what the heck are you talking about???" If the interviewer had asked "Would you like to access people and information all over the world from the keyboard of your PC?" you probably would have said "YES."

A PREEMINENT
BUSINESS
OWNER GETS
UPFRONT AND
PERSONAL
WITH HER
CUSTOMERS.

You didn't know the Internet would solve so many problems for you so you didn't know you needed it. The same is true for your products or services.

Your prospects aren't the expert and don't always have the words or knowledge to point you towards the solution.

If you ask the right questions, your customers can share what their problem is, what they need. Your job as the Preeminent expert is to translate that into the right product, service or solution and recommend their answer in words they can understand.

You stop pretending you already know everything about them. You stop arrogantly thinking that you know what makes them tick and what they want. You spend time with them, talk to them, develop deep relationships with them and ASK them about their problems, hopes and desires.

REALLY KNOWING YOUR CUSTOMER BEGINS WITH LETTING GO OF THE NOTION THAT YOU ALREADY KNOW THEM.

The market is always changing, people are always changing. So you have to adopt "beginners mind," reclaim some innocence and return to wonder. This literally creates some space for new information. It's just like having a bucket that's already full—you have to empty it before you can collect something else.

CURIOSITY CAUGHT THE CUSTOMER

So, what does your customer want? Be curious. Ask them what they want. Ask them about their life and their needs. Ask them what would make their life easier. Is there an innovative way that is more advantageous to the quality of the life? To their business? How could you dramatically increase the value? These questions are a great place to begin.

Then dig deeper and keep digging. As you get to know your customer, you're also going to start to hear *the things that they are not saying*.

You'll start to anticipate where they're heading and what they need to support them. You'll understand what they want so that you can lead them toward it on a route that will be more efficient, enjoyable, rewarding or less expensive than the way they've gone before.

When you know your customer that well and can provide that kind of value, they will love you. They will refer others to you. They can't help it because they're so happy and so grateful. Because you're giving them what they want and need, you'll start to attract all the customers you want.

This bears repeating: your customer probably doesn't know what she needs. But you can't sell her something she don't recognize that she needs. How do you make these two things come together, even though they seem in conflict?

Here's now you unite them. Very few customers are out shopping for a specific product or service. As a matter of fact, something like only 3 to 5 percent are shopping for a specific product or service at any given time. The other 95 percent to 97 percent are looking for ways take away their headaches or make their life better. They don't know that what you offer takes away their headache or makes their life better. When you understand their problem or need, you'll understand how to deliver the right solution.

As the expert, you also know that when you first get started, you can solve perhaps only part of their problem. Your objective is to first get them to work with you. Then you will build trust as you deliver a solution to your customer's great satisfaction. Now that you have their trust, you can introduce the rest of the solution that really, really solves their problem.

The only exception to this is when a customer arrives on your doorstep thinking they know what they need and they are totally wrong. You know they are wrong because you are the expert, you really do know more than the customer on this subject.

Let me give you an example. Recently, we delivered a marketing proposal to a prospect. They started taking the proposal apart. I'm sure that's never happened to you. This prospect took the proposal apart in such a way that the solution they were left with would not solve their problem. We told them that and politely declined their work as we know it would not meet their needs. Our leadership would not permit us to sell something to a customer that wouldn't work.

First things first: fall in love with your customers, *not* your business. Your business exists *only* to serve your customers.

- Ask them questions.
- Understand their problem as they see it.
- Provide them with an initial solution that addresses the problem they are trying to solve, not a problem they don't recognize.
- But sell them something that works, not just something to bring them in the door.

YOU ARE THE EXPERT

Do you see how intertwined leadership and a deep knowledge of your customer are? To lead effectively, you must feel confident about your expertise.

Do you know what you are an expert in?

While that might sound like a funny question, you'd be amazed at how many brilliant people get stuck answering it. Take a moment right now to ask yourself "what am I am expert in?" Then grab some paper and write down the areas where you know you are an expert.

Are you a master gardener, a phenomenal banana bread maker, a coach who helps the customer find the person they want to be, an equipment sales person who understands the spot-on right machine for the job, or an authority on helping single dads create better communication skills with their teenagers? Think about your business. In what areas of your business do you have authentic expertise?

The next step is to make sure that the area in which you have expertise is one that your customers value and want. If your customers don't want it and don't value it, then you've got a major disconnect. It could be that you need to shift your audience to a market that does value your expertise and will pay you for it.

You might find this exercise daunting. It's like asking a fish to describe water. We've been "in" it for so long that our expertise just feels "normal" and it's hard to see. It's also common to feel some embarrassment or hear negative self-talk. Your answers might feel boastful. They aren't. They are the facts about what you are uniquely skilled to deliver.

DIG FAR ENOUGH INTO YOUR EXPERIENCE, AND YOU'LL PROBABLY DISCOVER YOU'RE PREEMINENT ALREADY.

Mary was one who had difficulty identifying her expertise. She had been a nurse working with autistic children. As a matter of fact, her first experience began when she did social service through her school. She was 16. Yet when Mary decided to leave Corporate America to start her own care facility, she felt she had no preeminence she could claim. After all, all of her experience had come while working for someone else. Mary thought the best way forward was to hire someone with this expertise. Instead, we asked Mary to total all the hours she had spent caring for those children. She discovered she had over 90,000 hours. We asked her to call a school who trains nurses to work with autistic children to see how many hours they required someone could open a facility. The answer: Not many. Mary had more preeminence than most people in that field. What she didn't have was the courage to tell her prospects. Until she discovered she was Preeminent—already!

As you're digging, talk to your best customers. Ask them why they value your expertise. When you can articulate and "own" yourself as an "expert," you'll feel more confident and come across to your prospects as confident, as a leader.

You need confidence to show up as a powerful leader. Once you know your customer, have defined your area of expertise and determined that it's a match to what your customer wants and values, then it's time to LEAD. And I mean, LEAD like you've never LED before.

LEAD, LEAD, LEAD

Wrap your mind around this.

People love to be led.

And they particularly love to be led by qualified experts. Think about it. Doesn't it feel wonderful to find yourself in the company of someone who confidently knows how to do something very well and has your best interests at heart? It allows you to RELAX and enjoy the ride (or maybe get there more quickly or inexpensively or with a margarita, please). Thank goodness we don't have to be experts at everything. Thank goodness we don't have to figure it out all by ourselves. What a relief!

Imagine finding yourself alone and starving in the Amazon jungle with poisonous snakes, dangerous insects everywhere, wearing only the clothes on your back, dusk falling and utterly lost. Imagine that the kindly local shaman shows up, calmly speaks to you in your native tongue, offers you a sandwich, hands you a flashlight, and tells you he can guide you home safely if you just follow him through the jungle.

The world is full of customers who have problems that feel as dramatic as this, problems that you are uniquely qualified to solve. They can't wait for you to show up and say, "Hi. I understand where you are and I can help you get out of this situation. I've done it before and here's why you can trust me. **Follow me.**"

I SWEAR

"Lead your customers." That means you know what they want and you can get them to a great end-point. You don't sell them things they don't need and you don't sell them things just because they want to buy them. You also don't allow them to buy less from you than you know they need. That was our marketing prospect. That's not leadership.

Post this in your office and say it every day:

"I AM A LEADER!"

And here's your Oath to prove it.

Strategy of Preeminence
the oath of preeminence

I am my Clients Ultimate Trusted and Respected Advisor.

I have the responsibility and obligation to counsel my clients

in what's in their best interest,

to give them the best short and long-term results.

I will no longer accept or allow them to buy less than they should

or in fewer combinations than they should

or less frequency than they should.

I will never, ever, again

take an order because they are willing to buy.

You'll find this and all the worksheets and examples for you to download at
www.wideawakemarketing.com/resources

To get your copy, turn to the Resources at the end of this book for download instructions. Lucky you, you'll get this poster and the worksheets for upcoming chapters all at once.

[summary]

- Every great business follows a powerful leader.
- The first step in establishing a strong foundation for your business is to follow the rule of "Preeminence," which means "to stand out, have paramount rank or superiority; to have dignity and importance."
- To be successful, you must know and lead your customer. That's Preeminence in action.
- Get to really know your Prospects. Ask them questions, understand their problem or need before you offer any solutions.
- Never try to solve a problem your prospects do not believe they have. You'll be talking for a long time and they won't be buying quickly, if at all.
- Remember, it's highly likely your prospects don't really know what they want, what will solve their problem.
- Fall in love with your customers first, then your business.
- Identify your expertise.
- Take your Oath of Preeminence.

[exercises]

1. What kind of problems does your Ideal Prospect have? What are their needs? In their words, not yours.

   _____

   _____

   _____

   _____

2. For two minutes recite all the things you are an expert in. Have a friend write down what you say. Circle the ones most critical to your prospects and customers.

3. How did you react when you first recited The Oath of Preeminence? Did anything really resonant with you? Did anything put you off?

_____

_____

_____

_____

Positioning
CLAIM YOUR UNIQUE PLACE

Different. *Every business needs to be different in a useful and compelling way. Positioning your business—having it occupy a distinct space in your Ideal Prospect's mind—enables them to very quickly understand why they should choose you instead of everyone else who does what you do.*

Every business that excels has a distinct position that it "owns." Let's say you woke up this morning and decided you need a new car. You want a really safe car because your family is growing. If you want to buy the safest car you can, you're going to walk into the Volvo dealer because Volvo totally owns "safety." You may or may not buy the Volvo, but you are going to walk into the dealership. Others cars are safe, but Volvo centers everything they do on safety—and they tell you every chance they get.

Now here's the real, inside value positioning brings you: a successful business is a uniquely positioned business. Its market of Ideal Prospects understands and can repeat its position. If their Ideal Prospect does not

15

"get" who they are, their unique place in the market, then it's impossible for them to be chosen. They can throw a lot of money and precious energy at marketing and advertising but without clarity in what they own—their Position—it won't make a bit of difference.

Positioning contributes heavily to whether you win or lose. For example, three big companies wage war in the consumer market: Walmart, Target and Kmart. Walmart has become wildly successful by positioning itself around low-price. Their business is about creating the lowest price possible. They have constructed their entire business model to achieve low prices. They own low price, and we, their Ideal Prospects, know it.

It would be fool-hardy for Target to try to compete with Wal-Mart on price. They would probably lose. Target, instead, positions themself around "affordable style" (that's our description). Everything they do supports that position. They create affordable brands with trendy designs at great prices. And their business model is also built to deliver this position.

Then there's Kmart, at the bottom of the heap, struggling. They've tried many different positions but nothing sticks. Can you tell me what makes them special? And you can't say "blue light specials." That's from decades ago. Nothing comes to mind, does it?

Positioning is more than a niche. You won't succeed simply by choosing a great niche and great words to describe your niche. Great positioning means building everything about your business around your positioning. Wal-Mart has built everything about its business around creating low prices products. Target structured itself to create affordable, stylish brands. When you determine your positioning, you'll build your entire business structure around your positioning, too.

Great positioning cuts through all the noise of the marketplace.

Ideal Prospects are bombarded with millions of messages and bits of information every day. Just take a look at your e-mail in-box, not to mention media and advertising. To simply cope and function, our minds must compartmentalize all that data. If your business does not tell the marketplace exactly who you are and what makes you special, then you leave it up to them to decide. And, if you leave it up to them, you have no idea what "label" they're going to give you.

BE CLEAR ABOUT WHAT MAKES YOU SPECIAL, OR THEY'LL PICK THEIR OWN LABEL FOR YOU.

MASTER OF ONE

For a strong presence, don't be a "jack of all trades;" be a "master of one."

Successful positioning requires you to be very specific about what you do. To grow your business big, you need to target a very specific niche. In other words, you need to be small to get big. This is one of the biggest mind-benders you'll tackle as you grow your business. Most people want to do as many things as possible and target as many people as possible. We're asking you to do the opposite.

Winners do something very specific—like Volvo does safety—and target a very precise group of people who need that. When your positioning is specific, you can communicate it quickly and effectively. And in a market that gets noisier and noisier every day, you have fewer and fewer opportunities to be heard.

You want not only your most advantageous solution but also one that your Ideal Prospect seeks. Then you'll communicate this essential advantage very clearly, which means you must think "simple" not complicated. With clear, specific Positioning, you're set to dominate the market.

Our doctor friend, Bill, knew that most patients hated getting a bill from their doctor after a visit or hospital stay. They hated the bill because the amount of the bill was always a surprise. They never really knew what anything was going to cost. Bill decided to tackle just that in his new practice. Each of his services and procedures had a set price. Patients always knew before anything was done what it would cost them. Bill used this "predictable pricing" as the root of what made him different— his positioning. After all, how many doctors do you know who will share precisely the cost of their work prior to the procedure being done? Predictable pricing set Bill apart from every other doctor in his area, and he soon saw more of his Ideal Patients trooping into his office.

Positioning isn't hard—though it might feel like it at times. There are just a few decisions you have to make:

1. The first step, which we talked about in Preeminence, is knowing your customer or clearly identifying your "Ideal Prospect."

2. In step two you'll identify the problem your Ideal Prospect has. Why a problem? We'll share that with you shortly.

3. The third step is to articulate what makes you unique and separates you from your competition, also known as **"Differentiation"**— Positioning in other words.

4. In the fourth step, you'll identify the benefit your Ideal Prospect gets when they work with you—their take-away, what they put "in the bank."

YOUR IDEAL PROSPECT

Understanding your customer—really knowing who you're targeting— will make or break your marketing efforts (and possibly your bank account). Get your Ideal Prospect right and everything else flows. Get it wrong and everything in your business will feel like a chore.

Your Ideal Prospect needs services like yours, though they might not always recognize that what you offer is what they are looking for. That's your job. Your Ideal Prospect might already be showing up in your business and you just need more of them. Perhaps who is finding their way to you isn't who you want. That happens. Then you need to determine who you *do* want. Maybe your business is new and you're busy looking for anyone. Surprisingly, trying to market and sell to anyone will actually hurt your business more than help it, which is why you need to take a shot at profiling your Ideal Prospect: someone who can turn into an ideal customer, someone you really want to work with. One way to tackle this question is to craft a persona of a single person who would best exemplify your ideal customer. If you could create, right now, your Ideal Prospect, what would he look like, or would that be a "she?" What makes her "tick?"

The easy starting point for this exercise is to identify the age range of your Ideal Prospects. How specific can you be about the age group that you're serving? If you're talking to the "Echo Boomers"," young adults born in the '80s and 90's, you'll need to be very Internet savvy and comfortable using leading-edge technology because they've grown up with it. If you're talking to Gen Xers, born in the late '60s up to the 70's, you'll want to communicate in a way that honors their strong values toward individuality, remembering that this generation is prone to experimentation. The Baby Boomers, born in the 50's through mid 60's, are strong workers who value industry, staying fit, financial security, and family values above anything else.

What about other factors? What is their income and socio-economic level? Where do they live? Are you targeting a specific geographical area or the whole globe? What do they do for a living? What do they do for fun and recreation? What's most important to them? What are some characteristics of their lifestyle? Do they have children? Are they actively parenting? What is their education level? What kinds of problems, challenges, and issues are they dealing with? What keeps them up at night? What do they do on the weekends? What do they dream of doing or becoming?

Although it might seem a little crazy to figure out what your Ideal Prospects eat for breakfast every morning, the more intimately familiar you are with them, the more you will be able to help them solve their problems, speak to them in language they can understand, and communicate via methods that they utilize.

LA DIFFERENCE

What makes you unique? In marketing lingo, this is called "Differentiation" or what makes you different. It is the root of your Positioning. If you open up a shoe store, a chiropractor office, or a coaching practice and you're not clear about how you're different from everyone else out there, no one will pay attention to you. To put it bluntly, if you're just like everyone else, who cares? Do we really need another shoe store, chiropractor or coach? Nope.

Let's put this into play for a great shoe store. There are many shoe stores in town and you can get a pair of good athletic shoes at any of them. But let's say you're a runner. Having the right "fit" in a shoe could prevent a serious injury or take you to a whole new level of performance. You know you could get less expensive shoes at one of the chain stores but you go to the private store downtown and spend top dollar for new shoes. Why?

- They have a much better selection of running shoes.
- Their front-line people are experts who examine the wear on your old shoes to see how your foot rotates so they can recommend the right kind of shoe to compensate for that.

- They watch you walk in the new shoes to determine if the fit is right for you.
- They also have a selection of running apparel there so you can pick up some new shorts and socks while you shop.
- They offer you a complimentary electrolyte beverage when you arrive—a nice touch.
- They also have a runner's club, free local trail maps, and regular events for all skill levels so you can be part of your local running community.

There's no question, if you're a runner, that this is your place! You'll even pay a premium because you value this level of service and quality. That's differentiation. That's not the chain store at the mall. You can build your Positioning and center everything you do within your company on this attribute.

GET SPECIFIC. PROSPER.

Feeling nervous about "excluding" anyone? We've created Positioning for hundreds of customers and business owners so we can tell you: you're not alone. In fact, the newer you are to business or the more your business is struggling, the more frightening the idea of "Differentiation" can be. Business owners often say, "But I want to say 'Yes' to everyone; anyone can benefit from my service."

Although it might feel counter-intuitive, the bottom line is this:

If you try to be everything to everybody,
you'll end up being nothing to everyone.

Marketing is all about being specific. Sometimes that means a sacrifice in how you communicate.

Claiming your Position does not mean that you have to "turn away" customers who don't fit your target market if you really want them. On the contrary, you can take any customers that you want and, to meet your revenue goals, taking everyone who shows up may very well be the best choice.

But it does mean your *marketing messages* must communicate what makes you unique, which will be more meaningful to your Ideal Prospect and ultimately bring you more revenue not less. If you're doubting, trust us on this one.

"Something for everyone" confuses everyone, as this example from a behavioral economics experiment shows. A grocery store decided that having more options would generate more sales. So they increased the types of jam that they offered from 8 to 34. They made every conceivable variety of jam available to their customers. With all these choices, did sales go up? No. In fact, just the opposite occurred and sales declined. Why? Because having so many options confused the shoppers and they made the choice not to purchase jam at all. Researchers call this "buyer ambivalence."

TO EVEN SIT DOWN AT THIS TABLE AND BE A PART OF THE GAME WITH YOUR COMPETITORS, YOU MUST MEET CERTAIN CRITERIA WE CALL TABLE STAKES.

KNOW THE TABLE STAKES

Are your differentiators really different? Another mistake that people commonly make in the Positioning process is they list things as "differentiators" that are actually what we call "Table Stakes."

So depending on what market you're in, the stakes might be something like being certified, having an advanced degree, or having a piece of specialty equipment. **Table stakes don't make you different because all the other players who do what you do have the same ones.** It's a mandatory part of being in the game.

Here's the acid test for revealing table stakes: If you figure out what makes you different, write it out in a statement, and then replace your name with the name of a competitor. If the statement is still true, then it's not a unique differentiator for you.

Here are the qualities you *do* want in your differentiation:

- **It should be compelling.** You want to look for a twist on the usual formula, enough to make you stand out. For example, not just another coffee shop but the Adventure Café with the most unusual brews from around the world, a friendly parrot in the corner, world music on the air, extreme travel videos on the widescreen, and maybe a free lecture series with world travelers on Thursday nights.

- **It should be logical.** Make sure that the differentiator makes sense with your business and Ideal Prospect. Adding movie rental options to your pizza delivery service might make sense to your Ideal Prospect, a 20-something. Offering them "happy" plastic toddler toys with their pizza doesn't.

- **It should be useful.** A differentiating factor should be immediately recognizable as something of value to your Ideal Prospect.

- **It should be clear.** Keep it simple. When it's clear and simple then the market can remember it.

- **It should be true.** Make sure you can stand behind the differentiation and deliver positively on it.

- **It should be defensible.** At the end of the day, anything that makes your brand stand out should be able to significantly improve your business. Make sure to evaluate the cost with the benefit and monitor the efficacy of your endeavors.

READY, SET, DIFFERENTIATE

Figuring out how you are different requires you to see yourself not only as you are, but also as others see you. Get outside yourself and take a good look.

We've got a process to help you with that. Let's start by taking a look at what you'll be brainstorming. While brainstorming, let go of all your current ideas about what makes you different. No self-editing at this stage.

Differentiation

You can differentiate in five ways

Tangible				Intangible
What We Are	**What We Do**	**How We Do it**	**Who We Do It For**	**Why We Do It**

You'll find this and all the worksheets and examples for you to download at www.wideawakemarketing.com/resources

The left-hand side of the worksheet represents very "Tangible" ways you are different. As you move farther to the right, your ideas will become more "Intangible." That means that the items you list on the left are the most real, touchable. As you move all the way to the right, things become less concrete, but also more unique to you. And the farther to the right your go, the harder it is for the competition to follow you, as you'll see.

The first column, **"What We Are,"** is a highly factual description of who you are. It's more than just a description of the category you work in, such as coach, insurance broker, dentist and so on. You need to think about how to describe yourself a bit differently than others in your field. For example, you are a Type A Coach, or The Listening Doctor, or The First Time Seller's Realtor. While this column is very practical, it's the perfect place to position yourself if you are doing something no one has done before. When Yahoo launched the first Internet information portal, they positioned themselves as the first.

The second column, **"What We Do,"** captures the services or products that you provide and the benefits your Ideal Prospect gets from working with you. If you were a coach, you might list things like "I coach people through divorces. I relieve the stress that ties you in knots from divorce." You'll have lots of brainstorm entries in this column. If you make a unique product or provide a special service, this is a great place to find your positioning.

The third column, **"How We Do It,"** captures a process or "way" that you provide the product or service. For example, "We use only sustainable manufacturing processes," or "We have created a proprietary, experiential learning process." This is a particularly good place for those of you in a service business to find your differentiation because you might have a very unique methodology when delivering your service.

The fourth column, **"Who We Do It For,"** is about your Ideal Prospect. This is where you capture information about "who" your customer is. For example, "We create financial services for young families with children under the age of 6." We love to find what makes you different in this column, and not enough companies use it. Your customers might have very unique profiles or needs. If they do and you know them, you can build your differentiation on their uniqueness. In other words, their uniqueness becomes yours.

The fifth column, **"Why We Do It,"** really speaks to your passion, your vision, what compels you, what's in your heart, what likely sparked your desire to go into business. What makes this such a rich place to differentiate yourself rests in the fact that this is *your* passion—not your competitors'. Consumer-oriented companies seem more willing to position themselves on their passion than left-brained, business-to-business companies. That doesn't mean that if you're a left-brained business that you should avoid talking about your passion. Quite the contrary. We encourage you to spend some time on this column as it provides such extraordinary opportunities to separate yourself. We love Disney as an example. They position themselves on their passion—they put magic in your life. Everything from their theme parks to their short-lived breakfast cereal to Disney cruises is positioned as putting magic in your life. Disney competes with Universal but Universal doesn't put magic in your life. Immediate separation for Disney. And now you know why your kids tug at your sleeves to go there!

So once you start brainstorming, what might your ideas look like? Here are the ideas that came up for Vetrazzo when it first launched, a company that creates beautiful surfaces and counter tops made from recycled glass.

What We Are:
- Unique, visual solid surface using recycled glass
- Art from recycled glass
- The first distinctive, artful solid surface using recycled glass
- Best choice for self expression

What We Do:
- Create stunning, bold, lively, playful mixes
- Unique materials
- Enable personal expression of style and values in solid surface building materials
- Style that respects earth and environment
- Combine gorgeous and good into a single style
- Create solid-surface art work for homes and buildings
- Let your home or building tell story of who you are
- Put a story in every surface

How We Do It:
- Mixing bold, lively, dynamic pieces of recycled glass
- Patents
- Building to and beyond the standards of granite
- Recognizing that art/beauty lives in unique uses for reclaimed glass
- Recognizing that recycling affects local and global change

Who We Do It For:

- People who want to make a statement in their homes, buildings and world
- People who want to leave their signatures on their homes, buildings and world
- People who want to express their unique values

Why We Do It:

- Gorgeous and good
- Make a statement about you
- It's beautiful to do the right thing
- Sustainable WOW
- Nothing expresses your values like gorgeous and green

It's your turn to do the exercise. Write the five questions across the top of a landscape sheet to make your own worksheet, or turn to the Resources at the end of this book to learn how to download your own copy of ours.

THE TAKE-AWAY

It's time to face some truth—most of your Ideal Prospects are not even shopping for what you "make," and we use that word whether you make chocolate candies or your make consulting services. They most likely have no idea that they should be investigating what you do. Statistics show that only 3–5 percent of your Ideal Prospects are out shopping for what you make. What are the rest of your Ideal Prospects doing? They are looking for ways to take away their headaches or make their life better. They just don't know that you take away their headache or make their life better. It's your job to show them.

Therefore, the benefit that your Ideal Prospect is looking for is the specific relief they feel when you take that big, old headache away or you enable them to make their life better, as they've been trying and failing to do on their own.

Here's the kicker: most people spend their money on things that take away their headaches. If they have any money left over, then they do something nice for themselves. So you want your business to be the aspirin that takes away their headache, not the vitamin that makes something better, at least to start.

CRAFT YOUR POSITIONING STATEMENT

The next step in the Positioning process creates the really big excitement. You're going to determine which ideas on your Differentiation Worksheet are the strongest using a method created by Geoffrey Moore. Which ones are most important, most unique, most differentiating? Look for no more than four things that really demonstrate the essence of you.

30-Second "Elevated" Positioning Worksheet

For: (Target Customer)

Who: (state the problem)

We Are: (state your category and difference)

That provides: (key problem-solving capability)

You'll find this and all the worksheets and examples for you to download at www.wideawakemarketing.com/resources

Now take a look at those four—which one has the most power? Which one can you build your company on? Which one separates you the best from your competition? Take that one attribute and make it your differentiation/positioning attribute. Turn it into a sentence. This gives you what we call an "Elevated" Positioning Statement you can use as the foundation for the About Us on your website, marketing collateral and bios. While you will never recite this word-for-word, it provides you with the ingredients for your so-called "Elevator" Speech, or how you might answer the question, "What do you do?" in 30 seconds or less—about the time you might have if you were in an elevator with someone.

Your Elevated Positioning isn't about breathlessly telling someone absolutely everything about your business in a sentence. The key is to share something *compelling* enough to prompt further inquiry, a comment like "Wow, that's so interesting. Tell me more about that." The idea is to engage someone's interest and communicate what is unique and different about you, claim that "rung" on the ladder in their mind. If they are curious, then you can elaborate by talking more about the problems you solve for people, the benefits they receive from your product or service, and then "close" them on a next step or "Call To Action."

Watch your use of "I," "We," "Us," "Our," "Me" or "My." They distract the conversation from the Ideal Prospect's point of view, who ideally is the person you're talking to. And, of course, don't use jargon. Think of how many times you have asked someone the question, "What do you do," and you've heard a long ramble with ideas or concepts that make no sense to you. You probably felt bored

REMEMBER THAT THE KEY IS TO CONNECT, ENGAGE AND STIMULATE INTEREST. THE BEST WAY TO DO THAT IS TO BE CLEAR AND SIMPLE, AND MAKE IT MORE ABOUT YOUR AUDIENCE THAN YOU.

or even alienated and made the fastest excuse you could think of to move away from this person.

Here are some Elevated Positioning Statements that reflect good Positioning:

- "For women who want a primary physician with a natural approach to health and beauty, Dr. K. is "The Listening Doctor" who gets to the root cause of your problems."
- "Reverend J works with seekers who've been on the spiritual path for a while and are looking for clear activation steps to launch them into a new level of awakened personal success."
- "J M Designs creates exclusive, hand-made rings crafted by artists in developing countries for people who believe in beauty, the power of nature and making a difference in the world."

Now write a few paragraphs using the other three ideas. Those three also make you different, but even though they're not as strong as the one you choose for your Elevated Positioning, they'll help you weave a really strong story. They become your key messages built on the things that make you different. Now you have your "About Us" copy for your website and brochure.

Here's what our Dr. K wrote with her other ideas:

- For women who want a primary physician with a natural approach to health and beauty, Dr. K is "The Listening Doctor" who uncovers the root cause of your issues.
- A medically trained, licensed naturopathic physician, Dr. K seeks natural solutions to tackle the cause of health imbalances and to avoid dangerous side effects, using prescription medications only as the situation warrants.
- Whether you're dealing with raging hormones, fatigue, excess weight, or visible signs of aging, it's time to work with someone

who really listens to you and spends time with you. It's time to naturally return to the "me" you used to be.

Once you've chosen just the right words to convey your unique message, then practice, practice, practice saying it until it feels like a integral part of you. Then test it out on strangers, people who know you, as well as your customers and see what sort of response you get. Do they look fascinated, intrigued, curious? If so, you're on the right track. Do they look baffled, confused, or dazed? If so, ask for some feedback, re-work your message and try again.

Do not show people your Elevated Positioning Statement and ask, "I'm working on my Positioning—what do you think of this?" It's much better to try your message out on them and see what happens rather than to talk "about" it.

PUT A CHERRY ON TOP

By the end of your Positioning process, you'll be feeling confident and clear about your message. This is the time when a tagline might come to the surface as a clever or catchy way to capture your unique positioning.

We've noticed that business owners tend to obsess and worry about having the "perfect" tagline; they lose sleep and sometimes feel they can't move forward until they find the "Just Do It," "The Real Thing" or the "When it absolutely, positively has to be there overnight" phrase to capture the essence of their business message. We're here to alleviate your concerns.

We think of taglines as "a spice in the soup" or the "cherry on the top" of your marketing: nice but not critical. So if you come up with a good tagline, that's wonderful. Often taglines emerge over time. If you don't have one, it's not the end of the world. Trust that one will arrive when it's ready to and keep moving forward with your marketing and your message in the meantime.

UNSURE ABOUT YOUR POSITIONING?

Doing your own Positioning work can seem like becoming a surgeon, and then trying to operate on yourself—and without anesthesia. It's challenging to be so immersed in your business and also step outside and examine it objectively.

An objective eye from an outsider to your business might be just the ticket. We frequently provide positioning consultation to our customers. We interview you, take an objective look at your business, uncover the places where you're being too humble and craft the positioning document for you. If you'd like us to help, check the Resources section in the back of the book for our number and give us a call. Remember that this foundational aspect of your business is a critical first step in your marketing success.

[summary]

- There are so many businesses today doing the same thing that you must stand out by being different—usefully and compellingly different.
- The best way is to own a niche, something unique that you do better than anyone else.
- The keys to understanding your niche and what makes you different starts with studying your customers and answering four fundamental questions:
- Who are your Ideal Prospects? What is the problem they have that you solve? What makes you different and uniquely suited to solve that problem? What benefits do people get from working with you?

- Beware of Table Stakes. These are the things that everyone who is qualified to do what you do lists as attributes. Think of Table Stakes as your "dues" to enter your profession. Everyone in your profession has those same credentials.
- To simplify finding what makes you different, examine these five aspects of your business: Who We Are; What We Do; How We Do It; Who We Do It For; and Why We Do It.
- Among those five, find the most critical, the most important attribute you've identified. That's the root of your Positioning Statement—your Elevated Positioning.
- Avoid lots of "I," "my," "me" and jargon in your Elevated Positioning.
- Now practice, practice, practice your Elevated Positioning until it comes out naturally.
- Understand the difference between an Elevated Positioning and a tag line.

[exercises]

1. Who is your Ideal Prospect? List all the attributes that define the customers you're targeting.

_____

_____

_____

_____

2. What problem do they have that you solve?

_____

_____

_____

_____

3. What makes you unique and compellingly different versus everyone else who does what you do?

_____

_____

_____

_____

4. What benefit do people get from working with you?

_____

_____

_____

_____

5. Complete the Positioning Worksheet and address all five areas of differentiation:

Who We Are:

What We Do:

How We Do It:

Who We Do It For:

Why We Do It:

6. Complete your Positioning Statement:

_____

_____

_____

_____

Product Funnel
TRUST ME. TAKE THE LEAD

"Marry me." *Would you say yes to a marriage proposal after just one date? Probably not. After you ran away as fast as you could, you'd say, "Was she crazy? I barely know her."*

Your customers are no different. If you saw a big banner ad that said "Look Younger for ONLY $199" on the home page of a website you just visited for the first time, it's highly unlikely that you're going to whip out your credit card. Why? Because you don't have a relationship with the company yet. You don't trust them enough to feel comfortable taking a $199 risk and that you'll look younger for your efforts.

As a business owner, how do you develop that relationship? If the first thing you see is a FREE digital book on "10 Foolproof Secrets to Looking Younger Naturally," you might sign up for that. Maybe it would give you some valuable ideas and besides, you've got nothing to lose. If you enjoy the digital book and your experience with the company satisfies you, you might say "yes" to their next, gentle offer: a five minute video of a makeover using natural cosmetics, for example. If you like what you see, you might eventually buy their "Sampler Package" for $39 so you could test out some of the products.

In other words, you'll willing to go for a "cup of coffee" get-together with this company and then maybe a short, simple "date" to see if you like what they have to offer. If that goes well, you might buy the full size products, sign up for a weekend natural beauty retreat at a resort destination or buy a series of sessions with one of their personal natural beauty consultants. Eventually, you might become such a fan of this company that you tell all your friends and actively share your experiences on the company's blog site.

YOUR PRODUCT FUNNEL GIVES YOUR CUSTOMER A CHANCE TO GET TO KNOW YOU IN SMALL STEPS.

Now you're dating…perhaps seriously!

It might seem like a fairytale, but it's just an example of a company with a solid Product Funnel.

Small steps allay the fear of risk, which is particularly important if a prospect has found you without a referral or on the Internet where all kinds of strange and evil companies lurk. The next step in the foundation of your Customer Generator System is to get clear about your Product Funnel and learn how to lead your customers in a direction you both want to go.

LEADING LEADS TO LEADS

The Product Funnel creates the pathway of opportunities that you craft that are specifically designed to build trust and rapport with your customers. Like the funnel in your kitchen, the Product Funnel is wide at the top to gather all the leads you can. The leads may be coming from many sources: networking, referrals, social media, advertising and so on. When those leads arrive, you want to make sure that you capture them all and then guide them exactly to what they need now.

The average lead costs anywhere from $75 to $300 to attract—that's measured in money, time and effort. If you've spent all that to get them to come to your party, imagine how crazy it would be to ignore them or cause them to feel uncomfortable about working with you.

FOLLOW THE LEADER— FOLLOW YOUR PREEMINENCE

Having a strong product funnel means you show up as the LEADER, take your valuable prospect by the hand, and show them the easy and low-risk ways that they can start benefiting from your services immediately.

Remember that people love to be led, particularly when they don't know where they are going. They don't have the knowledge to map their path—whether that's choosing an shirt and tie that match or designing a website that works. By having a clear and strong Product Funnel, all the guesswork and confusion about what service your customer needs now and next melts away. You eliminate that common issue of "But I don't know how to start or what to do." Your prospect begins to see that you know the way even if they don't. You know how to help them get to the end point successfully and painlessly.

Did you know that it typically takes between five and twelve exposures to a business before a prospect typically decides to buy? It's pretty uncommon for a customer to buy the first time they "see" or "hear" an offer. Typically, we humans miss the request the first time it arrives. If we receive it a second time, it typically zooms over our heads. We may receive it again, finally notice it, but not remember. And so it goes. Then someone mentions it to us. "Oh, yeah, I think I saw something on that."

Someone else mentions it again, or maybe we read about it. Suddenly we say, "I keep hearing about that thing; I want to check that out."

Keep in mind that you're always going to be in this process of sharing value and establishing trust with your prospects and customers. That's how you move them deeper and deeper into your Product Funnel as they buy from you once, twice, four times…or more.

Product Funnel

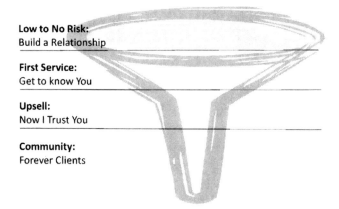

Low to No Risk:
Build a Relationship

First Service:
Get to know You

Upsell:
Now I Trust You

Community:
Forever Clients

You'll find this and all the worksheets and examples for you to download at www.wideawakemarketing.com/resources

EACH SUCCEEDING LEVEL OF CUSTOMER EXPERIENCE MUST BE BETTER THAN THE LEVEL BEFORE.

The Product Funnel starts at the wide top with the "no- or low-risk" ways that your potential customer can get to know you, and progresses to more valuable, higher priced services and products as you develop a more trusting and valuable relationship. The end goal is a Forever Customer—someone who is loyal to you and seeks you out for solutions to their needs in your category.

It's your job to lead the customer from one level to the next when they are ready and require that experience. If you're not clear what's next for them and what you want them to do, how in the world will they be able to figure that out?

Let's look at each level of the Product Funnel in more detail.

Level One: No-to-Low Risk—Build a Relationship

The products at the top of your Product Funnel, the wide end that gathers as many prospects as possible, must meet one key requirement—they **remove the risk of working with you.** You shoulder the risk so there's nothing or very little for your prospect to lose as they try you on for size.

Offer something of value to your prospect in exchange for their name, e-mail address and maybe their phone number that will go into your database. You want to give them a "taste" or a "sample" of what you do in a way that won't seem risky to your customer. You remove any barriers they have to giving your product or service a test drive. And once they say "Yes," you want to be impeccable with your delivery.

Nowadays the odds are good that this no-to-low risk offering arrives in digital format—a digital book, invitation to a special topic webinar, audio interview and the like—which requires delivery via e-mail. Therefore, the prospect must give you her name and e-mail address to receive the no-to-low risk offer. She does this by filling in the "opt-in box" on the home page of your website, or by completing a form you hand her if you are meeting in person, or simply by handing you her business card. She has just given you permission to continue the conversation with them.

Here's a little tip about humans. If you require a telephone number in the information they must provide, the odds are good that they will simply abandon the form. If you make the phone number optional, the odds are good that they will include it. Humans. We're funny people.

You have now achieved all you want from the top of your Product Funnel—the prospect has engaged with you at low-to-no risk to her, and you have information to continue the conversation with her.

No-to-low risk doesn't mean your offer must be free. You might charge for it. But you assume all or most of the risk if for some reason they don't see the results that you advertise. You see this commonly with money-back guarantees. We'll talk much more about unique ways you can reduce or eliminate risk in the Extraordinary Offer chapter.

Level Two: First Service—Get to Know Me

Now you've established some trust with the customer and perhaps they've sampled several of the products or services that you've offered them for free or at a very low cost.

THE KEY IS TO PROVIDE A "BRIDGE" THAT MAKES IT EASY FOR THEM TO ADVANCE FROM YOUR NO-TO-LOW RISK STUFF AND START GETTING READY FOR THE PRODUCTS OR SERVICES THAT CAN REALLY SOLVE THEIR PROBLEMS.

They're ready to work with you in a more meaningful way, and it's time to offer them some easy ways to do that.

A great way to get to know you is to offer affordable, low cost services. "Low Cost" means different things to different people and depends a lot on your business. However, asking the prospect to go from free to $500 is probably too big of a jump for most consumers, but it may not be too big at all if you're targeting business customers. If you're working with consumers, something in the $50 to $150 range would probably be attractive. At this level, the customer has experienced enough value that they're feeling confident about your ability to deliver benefits to them. Maybe they've seen results from implementing some of the ideas they got in your free e-book for example, and now they'd like to experience what you have to offer in a live tele-class or webinar. And they're willing to pay $49 to get that information.

Level Three: The Up-Sell—Now I Trust You

At this level of your Product Funnel, you have a base of customers who trust you and they're willing to pay for your products and services. Congratulations!

The next step is to introduce them to the "bread and butter" products and services of your business. These might be on-going coaching packages, workshops, training programs, full consulting services, or a complete website package. Here you offer your loyal customers your best and premium products. You are "upselling" them to the next level of problem solving because they are ready for it.

Level Four: Community—Forever Customers

The final stage of the Product Funnel is to create "forever" customers. Rather than just letting customers fade away, you use this level of the Product Funnel to keep customers engaged with you forever and ever.

These are the folks who love you, who think of you first, who will be with you for life. They've bought a number of products or services from you. They love, or at least like, what you deliver to them. They are an elite and valuable community to you, and you are a trusted resource to them. These customers are your source for great new ideas, innovations, and "graduate" level programs: your very own "Research and Development" team, if you will. These are the folks who are your best source of referrals, your advocates and the builders of your brand.

You need to determine what you can offer to engage your customers at the highest level and in an on-going fashion, if not an everyday way. Dentists often do a good job of this. When you leave their office, what do they do? They ask you when you want to set up your six month teeth-cleaning appointment. You don't leave their office without your next visit scheduled. And when you come back for that appointment, you have become a Forever Customer for that dentist.

Although it's obvious how valuable "Forever Customers" are, it's not uncommon for business owners to neglect them. Too often, entrepreneurs put all the focus on getting the leads into the Product Funnel. But if you get them in and then they fall right out the bottom, why bother? Yes, technically a funnel does have a hole in the bottom, but you're in more control of what goes out the bottom than you think.

THE REAL POINT OF THE PRODUCT FUNNEL IS TO GIVE YOU AND YOUR CUSTOMER A PATH TO WORK TOGETHER IN A LOGICAL FLOW FOR A LONG, LONG TIME BECAUSE YOU LOVE WORKING TOGETHER.

At this last level you definitely want to retain, support and foster community with these golden customers. Remember all the things the shoe store did to build a community of runners. Think about on-going ways you can make your Forever Customers feel that they are an integral part of your business—that they are special. Continue to add value.

Now we do want to state the obvious here—every customer does *not* need to go through every step of your Product Funnel. When you begin to talk to them about their problem or need, often you'll discover they are ready for your First Service or even the Upsell product.

That means beginning your work together at the spot they need you most, wherever it might be in the Funnel.

I'VE GOT GREAT STUFF.
HOW COME NOBODY'S BUYING?

If you have great products and services but no one is buying them, it's a sure sign that your Product Funnel is broken. You may be asking prospects to purchase too expensive an item before you've properly established trust with them. You're asking them to assume too much risk before they are ready. Maybe they are leaving you because they don't know the other, more advanced services, in your Product Funnel.

To make the Funnel work, you have to tell your prospects and customers about the next product or service that you offer. The Product Funnel gives you an on-going reason to communicate—a reason for the e-mail or the phone call. Never assume your customer knows everything that you do. They don't. Your job is to share that information when your customer is ready for that step.

Take a look at your current product offering and map it to the four levels of the Product Funnel. Where are you heavy? Light? Are you missing a level altogether?

The reason that the Product Funnel is part of your Customer Generator foundation is hopefully obvious to you at this point. It makes no sense to pound the pavement looking for leads or spend hours posting on social media sites only to drop prospects into a broken funnel.

When you clearly define your Product Funnel, then you can confidently lead your prospects to the level of product and service that's right for them. That inspires them to feel greater trust and confidence in you. If you continue to offer them increasing benefit and value, they will follow you to that golden land of "Forever Customers." And we call that a happy ending.

[summary]

- You can't jump right into "marrying" your customers. Think of it as dating and begin with a cup of coffee and gradually build to a long-term marriage.
- The Product Funnel is built to enable you to build credibility and then trust to create a customer who stays.
- Your job as a Preeminent Leader is to lead me through the Product Funnel, showing me what I need when I need it.
- More often than not, it takes five to twelve exposures before someone is ready to buy.
- The Product Funnel starts with "no-to-low risk" products and gradually builds to the "first sale," the "upsell" and the "the Forever Customer."
- If customers aren't buying from you, it's a sure sign your Product Funnel is broken!

[exercises]

1. What "no-to-low risk" products are you offering, or can you start offering?

_____

_____

_____

_____

2. What are your real "first services?"

_____

_____

_____

_____

3. What do your customers usually need next? What is your "upsell?"

    _____

    _____

    _____

    _____

4. What products enable you to create a "forever customer?"

    _____

    _____

    _____

    _____

Revenue Modeling
YOUR PATH TO CASH

Believe. *As a business owner, you get to work on your business. How amazing is that? You are living the dream that millions of people only dream about: you get to own and grow your own business. Most importantly, you don't have to figure it out by yourself or do it alone.*

Now you need to make sure it provides the business revenue to thrive.

Wendell was opening a new ice cream shop. Like most new entrepreneurs he was excited. And the area needed an ice cream shop as there weren't any in the area. Great location, wonderful ice cream… what more could Wendell need?

Wendell must have needed something more because his business didn't survive his first summer. What Wendell didn't know was how many ice cream cones he needed to cover his costs and make a profit for the business… and himself.

When we work with our customers on the next piece of the Customer Generator System Foundation, their eyes pop. Their facial expressions

WHEN YOU SEE HOW TO TAKE YOUR PRODUCT FUNNEL AND TRANSLATE THAT INTO REVENUE IN A RELATIVELY SHORT AMOUNT OF TIME, YOU'RE GOING TO FEEL EVEN MORE INSPIRED ABOUT YOUR BUSINESS.

change. Their posture straightens. It's safe to say they get really excited. If Revenue Modeling and goal setting makes you groan, you can relax because we're going to make it easy and fun.

While it might seem obvious that every business owner needs to chart their revenue targets and where that money will come from, you'd be amazed at how many owners just don't. How can you achieve your goals if you don't have them stated, and as importantly, written down? To achieve the success you seek, you have to know precisely what you need to achieve. Then you must manage to it. To manage it, you must measure it. Revenue modeling sets up your measures so you can manage to your goals, so you can achieve them.

WHAT ARE YOUR GOALS?

First things first; before we can show you how to map your revenue and achieve those goals, you have to have a goal to work with. You have to put a stake in the ground. How much money do you want your business to generate? What do you want your business to look like in18 months?

We gave up on three and five year plans a while ago—who can see that far into the future? That doesn't necessarily mean that they're not valuable. However in our experience working with business owners, life is moving so fast and shifting so quickly that 18 months delivers a more realistic time frame for most of us to work with.

These revenue goals you're about to set should be S.M.A.R.T., which stands for Specific, Measurable, Attainable, Realistic, and Timely, as Peter

Drucker started telling us in 1954. As you think about your 18-month goals for your business, keep the following in mind:

Goals must be Specific and Measurable.

The clearer your goal, the more inspiring it will be. Saying you want to "make more money" or "reduce debt" is vague. Saying you want to "make $20,000 a month by December 15 of this year" is specific and measurable. It leaves no room for interpretation. There's no question that you'd be able to measure whether or not you hit that goal by the end of the year.

Goals must be Attainable and Realistic.

Yes, of course anything is possible but if you start taking your first dance classes at 25 with the intention of being a prima ballerina in a major company, it's unrealistic to think that you'll be able to compete with the girls who've been dancing since they were three. The business just doesn't work that way. It's good to think big but not so big that you don't believe it's possible. That's counter-productive. For the same reason, any partners you might have must believe it's realistic too. That means when you have partners, goals must be *agreeable* and realistic.

Break your goal into attainable and realistic steps and phases so you can celebrate your success and build your confidence rather than falling short and risking the discouragement that may tempt you to give up on the goal altogether.

Goals must be Timely.

Certain goals have certain prerequisites. Eggs must be cracked open before they can be scrambled. A novice must go through certain initiations and devote time to practice before she can call herself a master. Make sure that your goal takes the natural sequence of things into account. Also make sure that your goal has a timeframe: a "by when?" date.

PLAY TO WIN

TAKING THE TIME TO DREAM ABOUT AND ARTICULATE THE GOALS FOR YOUR BUSINESS IS ONE OF THOSE 20 PERCENT ACTIVITIES THAT CAN GENERATE 80 PERCENT OF YOUR RETURN.

All business owners must face and overcome the tendency to work *in* their business instead of *on* their business. In other words, it's easy to become so busy doing, executing and making things happen, that they neglect to look up and steer the ship in the best direction.

S.M.A.R.T goals pull you forward, inspire you and connect you with the bigger vision of why you do what you do. They galvanize and motivate your team. They turn business into a game that's more fun to play because everyone understands the rules for winning. It's never any fun to play a game when the rules are unclear or always changing.

When we're clear about the goals, we relax. We enjoy the ride. We get curious and our intuition can guide us more powerfully toward the activities that will naturally put us in alignment with our vision. We begin to more powerfully harness the famous law of attraction.

Would it be okay with you if your business got easier and was more fun? **Of course.**

What are your goals for your business in the next 18 months? Then review them against the S.M.A.R.T model and edit them if necessary. Here are some questions to consider to get you rolling:

- What is working?
- What do you like doing?
- What are your biggest successes?
- What are your biggest challenges or failures?
- What are your customers' biggest challenges or needs?
- What is important to you?

- What is important to your customers?
- What engages your emotions, "lights your fire," or gives you the most energy?
- What engages your customers and lights them up the fastest?
- What do you feel most passionately about?
- What do your customers feel most passionately about?
- What kind of legacy do you want to leave?
- What's your intention with your business—sell it in two years, give it to your kids, work it until you retire?
- What are your financial goals for the business; revenue goal in the next 18 months?

THE MAGIC FINANCIAL FORMULA

Now it's time to take your 18-month revenue goal—how much money do you want to be making in Month 18—and show you the model for making that number a reality. Go back to your Product Funnel and look at the various products and services that generate revenue for you.

Revenue Modeling

Define your Target Revenue Goal:	Revenue Goal	18 Month (monthly goal)
		$10,000

Product or Service	Price
1) Coaching (hourly)	$75
2) Coaching (pkg.)	$450
3) Webinar	$249
4) CD/Workbook	$199
5) Group Coaching	$600

You'll find this and all the worksheets and examples for you to download at
www.wideawakemarketing.com/resources

THEN YOU
GET TO DO
SOMETHING
THAT WE
WISH WE HAD
LEARNED MUCH
EARLIER IN
OUR BUSINESS
CAREERS—PLAN

Now answer this question: what are the top four or five products in your Funnel that you know "make or break" your business? These may be the most profitable, most successful or most popular, but you know that they're the most important.

Write those top products in the left-hand column of your blank Revenue Model worksheet. Itemize the amount of revenue each of the past two months that you're currently generating from those products. This will show you, if you don't already know, exactly which products are producing the most each month now.

Planning your revenue—or anything—by working from the goal backwards, you create a straight line. You can see relationships like, "To get revenue from this product by Month 18, we have to have it launched by Month 15 and in the works by Month 12."

Revenue Model

	price	Unit	MONTH	Unit	MONTH	Unit	MONTH	Unit	MONTH	Unit	MONTH	Unit	MONTH
		#	1	#	2	#	6	#	8	#	12	#	18
Total Revenue Per Month													
PRODUCTS/SERVICES													

Planning backwards provides clarity not only in your revenue planning but in *everything* **about your business.** You can determine if that new and unforeseen opportunity is really an opportunity or a distraction. You can see when to say "yes" and when to say "no" to an activity. Planning backwards delivers a plan that's achievable.

Planning backwards might feel strange, but trust us, it fends off endless frustration. Most of us were taught to plan one month at a time, one foot in front of the other. Unfortunately, that doesn't provide clarity as you can only see a short space in front of you. It leads to a path that often looks like it was plotted by a bumblebee—heading over here and then over there and back again.

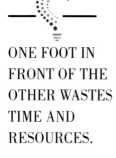

ONE FOOT IN FRONT OF THE OTHER WASTES TIME AND RESOURCES.

Take the Revenue Model and plot in how much money you want to make in Month 18 (for that month only). You've already entered the product prices. Now you determine how many you can sell in Month 18 and enter that in each column. How many more customers, packages, products or workshops would you need to add each month in order to work your way up to your 18-month goal? You don't have to do it all at once. You just have to add enough each month to gradually increase your revenue. What is your possible revenue for Month 18? You might be surprised. Many of our customers are. They discover that the Month 18 revenue target was just surpassed. Congratulations, you've just learned what your true potential is!

You might find that you want to adjust your goal or get more innovative about how you're generating revenue. If you're a consultant, for example, and your revenue goal of making $10,000 each month translates into more hours of one-on-one work than you want to do, then you can make adjustments to your Funnel. Maybe you want to try offering some group programs that you deliver through a sub-contract to increase your bandwidth and allow you to reach more people at one time. Perhaps you want to generate some passive income through affiliate programs or expand other revenue streams. Your revenue model is the place to experiment with these possibilities.

Revenue Model Sample

	$ Unit	Unit	MONTH	Unit	MONTH	Unit	MONTH	Unit	MONTH	Unit	MONTH	Uni t	MONTH
		#	1	#	2	#	6	#	8	#	12	#	18
Total Revenue Per Month			$1K		$2K		$4K		$6K		$8K		$10K
PRODUCTS /SERVICES													
Coaching	$75	3	$450	6	$900	6	$900	6	$900	8		12	$1.8
Coaching pkg	$450	0	$0	0	$0	6	$2700	6	$1800	4		4	$1.8
CD/Workbook	$199	3	$597	6	$1194	6	$1194	6	$995	5		5	$1K
Group Coaching	$600	0	$0	0	$0	0	$0	6	$2400	4		6	$3.6
Webinars	$249	0	$0	0	$0	0	$0	0	$1992	8		8	$2K
Total by month			$1047		$2094		$6786		$8387				$10.2

You'll find this and all the worksheets and examples for you to download at
www.wideawakemarketing.com/resources

The sample Revenue Model shows the various products and services for a coaching business, the revenue each one generates and how the whole model builds to the 18-month goal.

When you complete your Revenue Model, much will become clear to you. Are you working more hours than you want to? Do you need some new products or services? Is it time to adjust your pricing? Are you putting energy toward the 20 percent of your business that generates 80 percent of your profits or are you "spinning your wheels" doing things that don't move you toward your goals?

Your Revenue Model will also tell you a lot about your sales cycle. For example, if you know that you want to consistently add five new customers to your practice every month to reach your goal, then how many leads must you have to close five new customers? Do one out of ten prospects typically hire you? If so, that tells you that you need to talk to at least 50 new prospects every month. Easy!

Although you might love a good mystery, you probably don't need it in your marketing. Revenue Modeling takes the mystery out of your marketing and reveals exactly what you need to do to get where you want to go.

[summary]

- Business revenue enables your business to thrive. So let's plan to thrive.
- Revenue Modeling is about setting goals—not five years out into the unimaginable future, but an 18-month goal that you can see and feels real.
- Goals are S.M.A.R.T.—specific, measurable, attainable, realistic and timely.
- Remember the more you work "on" your business rather than "in" your business, the faster you can grow because you'll be focused precisely on the most important things your business needs you to do.
- Determine your business goals 18 months out from today.
- Start by determining how much money you want to be making in month 18—not how much per year, but how much in that 18th month.
- Now list all your products and services and their prices.
- Plan your way backwards from Month 18 to Month 14, Month 12, Month 9, Month 6, Month 3… today. How much of each product and service can you sell? How much do you need to sell?
- Now you can "see" what you need to sell, what services you need to create, and when you'll meet your revenue goals.

[exercises]

1. What are your goals for your business in Month 18?

   _____

   _____

   _____

   _____

2. Examine whether they are S.M.A.R.T goals by asking, "Are they Smart, Measurable, Attainable, Realistic and Timely?"

3. Complete the Revenue Model for your business using the form you can pick up as described in the Resources section at the end of this book.

Extraordinary Offers

SO GOOD, THEY'VE JUST GOT TO SAY "YES"

Risk. *The only people who really like it are those crazy thrill seekers like Evel Knievel who get paid a whole bunch to swallow risk in huge gulps.*

Believe me, your prospects don't like risk. "Normal" people try to avoid risk as much as possible, or at best they want to feel like they can manage the risk they're about to gulp down. I know you don't think so, but most of your prospects believe that saying "yes" to work with you or buy your product is risky.

Here's the math on that: Customers don't like risk. You are risky. Customers don't like you.

At least until you eliminate the risk.

Risk exists in that very first "yes" because they don't know you, don't know your products or services, don't know if you'll deliver what you say, don't know if they'll be happy with their choice. They just don't know. Too many things are unknown no matter how many references or assurances

THE BOTTOM LINE: PERCEIVED RISK STOPS YOUR PROSPECTS FROM BUYING FROM YOU.

you provide, particularly if they found you on the Internet where all kinds of evil lurk.

Your job must start with convincing the prospect that you are a safe choice. You put testimonials in your proposal or on your website. You hand over references that will surely sing your praises. You work very hard to make your prospect feel comfortable so they can utter that one, precious word…"Yes."

There is one thing you can offer that tantalizes and attracts your prospect, one thing you can do that you're probably not doing—and your competition surely isn't doing—that will eliminate their risk and get that magic word out of their mouth.

MAKE AN EXTRAORDINARY OFFER

An Extraordinary Offer tantalizes your prospective customer and makes it much easier to say "yes." An Extraordinary Offer moves all or most of the risk of saying "yes" that first time off the shoulders of your prospect and on to yours.

An Extraordinary Offer changes our math equation: Customers don't like risk. You aren't risky. Customers like you.

AN EXTRAORDINARY OFFER DOES PRECISELY WHAT WE WANT IT DO—CREATES AN EASY "YES."

Your prospect utters "yes" faster and with greater confidence. They see your difference immediately. They begin to work with you or purchase your product with assurances that if all is not as advertised, they have some recourse.

An Extraordinary Offer isn't just a great deal for your prospect. It's a fabulous deal for you, too. Now you stand out from the noise and clutter in your marketplace. How many people do what you do or offer a similar product to yours? Yet the odds weigh in your favor that your competition doesn't make an Extraordinary Offer. Go check them out and see for yourself. In a sea of financial planners, life coaches, yoga instructors, dry cleaners, health and beauty products, consultants, spiritual therapists, candy makers—whatever your business does—an Extraordinary Offer creates immediate separation from all the other businesses who do what you do.

The final Foundational piece of your Customer Generator System, the Extraordinary Offer, delivers one of the simplest methods of getting to Yes, turning a prospect into a customer, separating you from your competition and adding tons of value to your new customers, all at little cost to you.

REMOVE THE BARRIERS TO "YES"

You see Extraordinary Offers every day. You've probably even succumbed to their power more than a few times.

100% Money-back Guarantee.

Try the product for 30 days. If you don't like it, return for a full refund.

Test the mattress in the comfort of your own home for 30 days. If you are not completely satisfied, call us to arrange for pick-up and a full refund.

See how they switch all the risk from the prospect to the seller? These examples of Extraordinary Offers are tried and true, and they work. How many Sleep Number beds have flown out the door due to the money-back guarantee and free pick-up offer above?

At first a money-back guarantee seems scary many small business owners. They worry about their risk. "What if everyone sends the product back? I can't afford to restock and give back all that money. Now I'm losing!"

Watch how that worry evaporates. First, you are undoubtedly offering a product that you love, other customers have loved, and you know it works. You've tested it, used it yourself and sold it to others who find it irresistible. If you aren't offering an intentionally flawed product, what are you worried about? If you need a little more reassurance that such a guarantee won't put you out of business, statistics show that on average only 2 percent of products are ever returned. Once people get the product and start using it, their worry about risk dissolves. Then there are the folks who just never

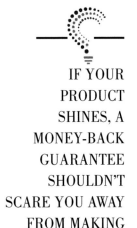

IF YOUR PRODUCT SHINES, A MONEY-BACK GUARANTEE SHOULDN'T SCARE YOU AWAY FROM MAKING SUCH AN OFFER.

get around to returning within the allotted time period. We all have that bottom drawer of products that just didn't quit hit the mark.

Money-back guarantees do come with a couple of considerations. As highly effective as they are, they've been done a million times, and our ears don't "hear" the offer as crisply and cleanly as something new. Test this for yourself. When a company makes a money-back guarantee offer, do you hear it? Do you see it? Or do your eyes glaze over while you hear only "blah-blah-blah?" With so much competition in the market creating so much noise and mayhem, a money-back guarantee offer just might be too commonplace to truly stand out.

If you're in the service business, a money-back guarantee must be framed properly as a service offering is by its nature more subject to interpretation than a product. What precisely does "satisfaction" mean when you're a consultant delivering a program to a customer, a life coach working as a sounding board for a customer or a spiritual therapist advising a member? Satisfaction becomes much more difficult to define as each individual has a different definition of what satisfaction means to them. No matter what the initial proposal says, a money-back guarantee for a service requires a very tightly defined end-point.

You could deliver precisely what you promised yet your customer isn't satisfied. Your definition of service completion and your customer's don't match but you don't know until you reach what you think is the end. No one, not you or your customer, wants to find themselves in that situation.

The good news is Extraordinary Offers come in many different shapes and sizes, not just the 100 percent, money-back kind. You'll find lots of inspiration for your Extraordinary Offer here.

FREE: THE BRIGHT SHINY OBJECT

The word "free" causes rational people to do some extraordinary things. That's why we call "Free" a bright, shiny object.

You've probably done some amazing things for a "Free" something.

I know I have. Several years ago, before the Christmas holidays, I was on Amazon shopping for a book. I found the book I wanted and went to check out. Up popped a message. "Free shipping for orders over $35." My order totaled only $16.95, the cost for the one book, but not enough for free shipping. Suddenly I didn't want to pay for shipping anymore when someone else could get it for FREE!! I marched down the hallway and into the family room, asking who needed a book. I was on Amazon, and this was the time to order if you had a book you needed to buy. No one responded.

FREE CAUSES PEOPLE TO TURN THEIR HEADS AND GET HYPNOTIZED, AND DO SOME UNBELIEVABLE THINGS.

Irritated because no one needed a book I turned and marched back to my office and promptly scoured the Amazon book collection, looking for a second book. I found one and placed it in my shopping cart. Now I had FREE shipping. I was so pleased with myself. Hours later when the drug of FREE wore off I knew that FREE had cost me money. Shipping cost $3.95. The second book cost $15.95. I spent $15.95 to save $3.95 and was pretty darned proud of myself for that transaction, too. Yet it cost me $12. And by the way… I never have read that second book.

I tell you that story because I know I'm not alone. I'm not the only one hypnotized by the Power of Free. And not the only one totally pleased with myself over the transaction. You've done it, too.

For example, have you ever…

- Stopped by a food stall for a free sample and then bought the item?
- Listened to a presentation at a trade show to get the tee shirt and then got interested in their product?
- Picked up a free coupon for a product you don't use and then used the coupon "just to see?"
- Used the free calendar some random realtor sent you and then called them about buying or selling your house?
- Stood in the very long line for free Ben & Jerry's ice cream on their once a year Free Cone Day? And then paid for a second scoop??

IF FREE WERE A VIRUS, WE WOULD ALL BE INFECTED.

Can we just say it? Free makes us happy. More importantly, FREE makes your *prospects* happy. So happy that they will say "yes" when that might not have been their intention. Free reduces risk just about as far as anything can.

Free Offers

Buy Two—Get One Free

Dog Walking— On time, every time or you get a 50 lb bag of dog food *free*

There are probably a lot of reasons why Free created unexpected behavior in our prospects. One stands out. In every purchase there is an upside and a downside. The downside is called risk that things might not turn out as the purchaser planned. We saw that above in our discussion of money-back guarantees. With free the downside is eliminated, or at least the perception of a downside is eliminated. All that's left is the upside, and the upside starts to blossom in its radiance. When the upside is no longer counter-balanced by a downside, the upside swells in desirability.

The Land Of Free means we don't have to take apart the offer to find the "got cha." Free isn't just a different way of saying "come and get a discount." It's a Land all by itself.

Which means a faster, easier "yes" from your prospects.

Don't you just love Free?

LAYER ON THE VALUE

Suppose neither of the Extraordinary Offer types offered above strikes your fancy or just don't appeal to your Ideal Customer. You can create an appetite to say "yes" in another way.

Add lots of great value to your offer.

If you're up in the wee hours of the morning, you've seen examples of these Extraordinary Offers on late night TV.

Buy the Slap Chop™ for only $19.95 and get the second one FREE!

But wait there's more!! Order now and you also get—not one but two—Graty Cheese Grater included. All of this for only $19.95.

Now you don't have to be as cheesy (pardon the pun) as the Slap Chop offer, just pay attention to what they are doing. They establish the value of the primary product, in this case $19.95. Then they begin offering other valuable incentives without changing the price. Surely, you now have a great deal! All those extras for Free (there's that word again).

One company we've worked with layered on value by taking their primary offering, coaching at $395 a month, and coupling it with a 4-part webinar that usually costs $195 and their $29.95 workbook. Normally, this offer would cost $619.95 but the whole package is bundled together for the same low price as coaching—$395.

Layer on the Value

**Workbook&
Webinar only
...plus
Consultation.
Normally $996.
Now only $397!**

**Manicure &
Pedicure—
only $35...plus a
15 minute
massage**

If we peel back the covers on this offer, you'll discover that offering the bundle at the same price as coaching alone doesn't cost the company any more money. The webinar is recorded. It takes four hours of her time, and she can provide it over and over again without any additional time invested. The workbook is digital. Once the product is written and produced in digital format—which can cost virtually nothing if you do it yourself—it doesn't cost a thing to make or ship. The cost of offering coaching and the cost of offering the bundled package is practically the same. Yet prospects perceive greater value—they are getting so much more for their $395!

Look at all your products and services. How could you bundle them to create greater perceived value for the prospect without extensive additional costs to you?

We all love a deal. So offer your prospects one.

OFFER THE UNEXPECTED

We see one other type of Extraordinary Offer that delivers an easy "yes" from a new prospect.

Offer something your competitors don't.

You've seen this one on TV.

Knives that never need sharpening. Never buy another set of knives again!

What a promise—particularly if it's true! Doesn't this separate these knives from all the other ones out there?

You'll find it by looking at the places that everyone thinks are "givens"—that's just the

THIS TYPE OF EXTRAORDINARY OFFER IS BUILT BY RECOGNIZING SOMETHING THAT MOST COMPETITORS IN YOUR MARKET DON'T OFFER AND CUSTOMERS REALLY WANT AND YOU GIVE IT TO THEM.

way it is. Prospects and customers think, "that's just the way it is" but would line right up if there was a different offer out there.

Once you find this unfulfilled need, you fill it. In very simple terms, if every competitor comes out the door and turns right, what would happen if you turned left? There are prospects dying to work with someone who turns left if only there was someone.

Unexpected Offer

Realtor— Love the Home You Buy or I'll sell it for *free*

Worker's Compensation Report – We'll Find the Money You're Wasting FREE

One of our customers is an attorney. Have you ever worked with an attorney? One of the things people dislike about them is the painful surprise they receive when they open their bill. You know how much the attorney charges per hour, but you have no idea how many hours they worked—until you open the bill. Rarely do you see a smile at bill-opening time. No one likes surprises like this, yet this is how attorneys price their services. With our assistance our customer recognized that opening the bill was one of the top reasons people don't like working with attorneys. Together we looked at all his services and created fixed prices for all of the services a customer is likely to need first. His Extraordinary Offer became "Always Predictable Pricing; Never Be Surprised by Your Attorney Bill Again." His business exploded.

He did the unexpected. He tackled head-on a problem that the market has when working with attorneys, a problem that was a "given," a problem that everyone—except him—felt they had to live with. You know… that's just the way it is. He turned left instead of right, and there were armies of prospects who were thrilled and relieved to find him.

Try this one. What if you had a dog walking service, and you knew that a common complaint about dog walkers is they don't arrive on time? What if you knew that dog owners groan when hiring a dog walker because they have to deal with the poor pooch whining mercilessly at the door because You-Know-Who is late again? You turn left instead of right. Your Extraordinary Offer: "On time, every time or you get a FREE bag of dog food."

Now the owner really doesn't want the free bag of dog food. They want their pooch walked. But the offer's underlying message is "We'll be there on time." If you had a choice between a dog walker who made you such an offer and one who made no offer, which would you choose? Right. The one who backed up their service with an Extraordinary Offer and showed they truly mean what they say.

There are a lot of dog walkers who advertise on-line. With this offer you stand out, and not just because most don't make any Extraordinary Offer. You're addressing an issue on the mind of your prospect. You'd be a star.

WHAT'S THE COMPETITION DOING?

Look around at your industry and check out what your competition presents as their Extraordinary Offers. Check out their websites or give them a call. If you're like many of our customers, you're not going to find much out there.

What could you offer your customers to catch their attention and make you different from everyone else in the pack? What gets in the way or stops your customer from buying from you? How can you remove that risk for them? What are you willing to stand behind?

Keep in mind that the average return rate on products is less than 2 percent. For example, if you offer a can opener that promises never to leave sharp edges or "simply return the product for a full refund," only 2 percent of those can openers will come back. Of course, we recommend that you make offers only that you can stand behind.

OFFER NON-THINKING DECISIONS

Extraordinary Offers must take into consideration how your prospect's mind works. We like to think of ourselves as very rational beings, making the smart selection. When it comes to purchasing, however, we make strange choices.

Your goal, always, is to create a non-thinking decision to get that easy "Yes." You get the brain involved, and humans do funny things.

Suppose you are given the choice of receiving a FREE $10 gift certificate toward something you want or a $20 gift certificate but you have to pay $7.00 for it. Which would you choose?

We make this offer all the time at our workshops just as a test. Here's what this unscientific experiment proves each time. People overwhelmingly chose the free $10 certificate. They perceive it to be a better deal even though the second option would actually give them $13 toward what they want to buy. But what really happens is they don't have to think about the free certificate, and look for the loop holes. The offer is what it is. When we make the $20 certificate offer and you pay $7 bucks, we create a thinking decision. Worse yet, we create a decision that requires math!

The first offer not only presented something for free—and we already know Free is a magical place—it created a non-thinking decision.

There was no reason for the prospect to engage their brain to decipher the offer. The offer was completely clear and easy to understand—a non-thinking decision.

At every turn and in every way we want to create an easy "yes." Take their brains out of the choice.

Remember in developing your Extraordinary Offer it's all about perception. Your customer must perceive that they're getting a deal and receiving something out of the ordinary that's valuable to them. This requires you to really get in the mind of your consumer. What would make your product

IN ADDITION TO SHIFTING THE RISK FROM THE PROSPECT TO YOU, SHIFT THE THINKING FROM THE CONSUMER TO YOU.

or service irresistible? Yes, it must solve a specific problem and delight your customer. All things being equal, what would make your solution more enticing than all the others out there? What we know for sure after coaching thousands of business owners, is that having a strong Extraordinary Offer will absolutely set you apart from the noise.

[summary]

- Create an Extraordinary Offer for your business.
- Your goal in the offer is to remove the barriers to "Yes."
- Offer ideas include: money-back guarantees, Free products, added value, and offering the unexpected.
- Check out your competition to see if they are making an Extraordinary Offer.
- Your second goal is to take the prospect's brain out of the decision-making process.

[exercises]

1. Visit the website of ten competitors. Notice how they present their products and services. Do they make any Extraordinary Offer? Are the Extraordinary Offers the same or similar (then they aren't irresistible any more, are they?)

2. Draft ideas for an Extraordinary Offer for your business in each of these categories. Choose three that meet the two goals of removing barriers to "yes" and creating a non-thinking decision. Try out each of the three with your prospects. See which is most appealing.

   - Money-back Guarantee: _____
   _____
   _____
   _____

   - Free Offer: _____
   _____
   _____
   _____

   - Layer Value: _____
   _____
   _____
   _____

   - Do the Unexpected: _____
   _____
   _____
   _____

PART TWO

The Customer Activators

You've got the foundational requirements of your business firmly in place.

Now it's time to activate your business. You're ready for new leads... which will lead to new customers. Are you ready to double or triple your customers? Start seeing your new success because in the next section, Activation, everything in your business changes for the better and it changes *FAST*.

The Power 100
YOUR KEY TO GROWTH

Connections. *We all love them. And you've got them—far more than you think.*

What we find as we work with customers is that far too many want or hope that customers will just contact them. Some business certainly happens that way. But a thriving business cannot be built on chance. It's built on a strong plan—and execution. Now that you've completed The Foundation in Section 1, you've got that strong plan.

The next steps are the execution. We call them Customer Activators.

You already hold in your hand the key to having all the customers you've ever dreamed of. The success you're working for isn't "out there" but is held right there in your own hands. The Power 100 exercise uncovers your key.

In many cases you already know them. The Power 100 is a list of your best customers, key

THE POWER 100 REVEALS THE TOP 100 PEOPLE WHO CAN ELEVATE YOUR BUSINESS.

prospects, influencers, power-players and prospects who will either hire you directly or put you in touch with others who will.

The Power 100 might just be the most incredible Activator of all. Every customer we've worked with who created and used their Power 100 elevated their business, and several did it in the face of a recession.

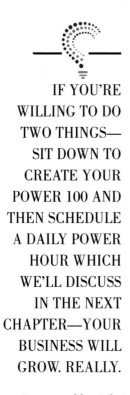

IF YOU'RE WILLING TO DO TWO THINGS— SIT DOWN TO CREATE YOUR POWER 100 AND THEN SCHEDULE A DAILY POWER HOUR WHICH WE'LL DISCUSS IN THE NEXT CHAPTER—YOUR BUSINESS WILL GROW. REALLY.

Two years ago we were working with a customer who specializes in weight loss, creating amazing results for his customers. Ed had a good business. But he was on a mission. Ed was totally dedicated to enabling every overweight person to reveal the true person within. He wanted to reach out and touch more and more people in need. But he didn't know how to grow. We introduced him to the Power 100. Ed found a quiet place and sat down to create his list. One year later he had doubled the size of his business. And not just any year—the year the economy imploded!

While Ed was dedicated, there is nothing that he did that you can't do. Ed had no tricks, no secrets, no inside approach to finding new customers. He only had his Power 100.

For you, like Ed, it only takes 100 to start. Don't let that number intimidate you. Using our Power 100 methodology, breaking down the list into five distinct parts, you'll have more than 100 names in no time.

WHO MAKES THE LIST

Like Ed, you'll find your Power 100 by examining five categories of people and companies.

1. The first and most obvious are the people—individuals or in companies—who you know. You can pick up the phone and call them. You're pretty sure they need what you do. Maybe they've worked with you before. Perhaps they have discussed their need for products or services like yours with you or a mutual friend. The point here is you know them and believe fully they should be working with you. Call them your direct prospects.

2. The second group is created from people who have already sent you referrals or could provide you with them. These folks might have already worked with you or might have referred others to you. Maybe they have a large network of friends or business associates, great contacts or a big database. Maybe they just are natural connectors. They are your friends, former customers or people who just love what you are doing—anyone who has or could refer you to your Ideal Customer. They are your Walking Evangelists and need to be cultivated.

3. The third category includes those who *could* be working with you—individuals and companies—**even though you don't know how to reach them right this moment**. They are your indirect prospects. Don't worry right now that you don't know them or how to reach them. Just list their names or the names of their companies. You can do your investigative work later. This is the main point about this part of your Power 100 list making: based on what they do, you're pretty sure they would be a good candidate for your services.

4. The fourth group is created with people and companies with whom you could joint venture. You believe they would be open to offering your services to their customers. In return they get some of the revenue. Ideally, these folks already have "your"

customer and offer complementary, but not competing, services. For companies just starting out, this is one of the fastest ways to build your business, using other people's customers to grow your business—with their permission, of course.

5. The last category comprises your **Wish List**. In your wildest dreams, who would you like to work with? Come on! Let loose. Let your imagination have some free rein. Whatever you do, don't blow off this category as silly or impossible. One of our customers put Oprah Winfrey on her list. She was invited to write a periodic column for *Oprah* magazine. That might not be Oprah, but it's pretty darned close. When you recognize who is on your Wish List, the odds of you finding them, or them finding you, increase more than you can imagine.

DOES IT HAVE TO BE 100?

Yes, it has to be at least 100.

One hundred is a magic number that works time and time again. It's large enough to create momentum, and small enough that it's not too overwhelming to create.

If your internal saboteur is rearing its ugly head at this moment and telling you that 100 is an insurmountable number, calmly thank it for its point of view and tell it that you're moving forward anyway. Lots of business owners and sales people before you have gotten over this perceived "I-can't-do-it" limitation. It's a contest between your internal saboteur and the part of you that knows you can succeed. Who do you want to win this battle?

If you need one more encouragement, realize that the average person has over 250 names in their e-mail address book. There will be lots of great possibilities in that list to get you rolling.

CREATE YOUR POWER 100 LIST

First, you need a place or formula to capture your Power 100. If you already have a contact management system or spreadsheet program, you can use that. Here's an example.

Power 100

Names	How They Can Help	What You'll Ask Them To Do	When You'll Contact Them

You'll find this and all the worksheets and examples for you to download at www.wideawakemarketing.com/resources

The sample shows the columns you need most. The first column lists the name of your contact person. You've already completed this column based on the work you just did above.

Now the second column weighs how each can help you, how "hot" or interested you think they might be. Enter "A, B, C, or W" to categorize each prospect.

- The "A" list includes the very hottest prospects. These are folks who already love what you do or who have purchased from you before. They could come from your direct prospects, referral or even joint venture list. You know them and can contact them quickly. These are your best prospects. If they became customers, they would significantly impact your success.

- The "B" list holds your "warm" prospects. These leads need some development. The relationship needs to be groomed, or they would be good for your business but you don't yet know if they'd be great. They have the potential of moving fairly quickly to the "A" list. These prospects would most likely come from your referral, joint venture and maybe even your indirect prospects list.

- The "C" list would be the coolest leads, the one's you're least sure of or need the most development. They probably come from your indirect prospects, joint venture and wish list lists. Your job is to do some digging to get more information on them, learn more about the company and understand their needs. Also, you want to investigate their most likely person you should contact to begin a conversation with them.

- The "W" stands for your wish list prospects. Maybe even some of your joint venture prospects are wishes. Don't underestimate the power of intention. Write down your desire. You'd be amazed how often impossibilities become realities. Who do you really wish you could work with? Who would be an absolute "coup" for your business? Although it might seem out of reach or you may have no idea how to make it happen, who would you ideally like to have as one of your customers? Dream big.

Add columns to contain the other information you need. You also want your prospects' contact information on your Power 100, and you want a column to track your progress with them: when you called, when you agreed to follow up again, what you spoke about, and any actions you promised to take. It's mandatory that you keep track of all these details in order to develop a solid relationship. It's also important for you as a business owner to keep track of how many times you typically connect with a prospect before they become a customer. Does it take five calls, ten or fifteen? This is valuable information for you to know for future planning.

You may also want a column for gathering information about their referral power. For example, how large is their database or network? A satisfied customer who has a database of 50,000 people has considerably more referral power than someone who also thinks you're fabulous but only knows a few hundred people.

WHERE DO I FIND MY POWER 100?

Once you've got your Power 100 Capture Sheet format ready to go, it's time to start populating it with contacts. You actually know a lot more people than you think you do.

- Start with your e-mail contact program and see whose contact information you already have.
- Consider the associations and professional organizations you belong to.
- Search through your on-line social and professional sites like Facebook, Twitter, and LinkedIn. What other on-line communities do you frequent?
- Go back into your old customer files.
- Think about the different roles you play in your life: family, alumni, friendships, parenting, hobbies, activities, organizations, affiliations. There are probably people in all areas of your life that have the kinds of challenges that your business can solve.
- If a category of companies dominates your list—pharmaceutical, manufacturing, retail services—go to your Yellow Pages, search

on-line or get association lists to gather the information you need to make a good connection.

JUST DO IT

Once you begin to fill in your Power 100 list, it generates momentum all on its own. You begin to think of more and more people and they, in turn, connect you to even more. Trust your internal guidance and follow those inklings and nudges from your intuition. As you do that, your contact list expands more and more effortlessly.

Here's another inspiration for you. Using the Power 100, Georgie doubled her practice. She concentrated on people who could refer business to her. So much of her business had come to her this way, but she had never "encouraged" those referrals. Stepping up to the Power 100, Georgie discovered that people *wanted* to refer business to her. She only needed to encourage them and share what needed to be said. Most importantly, Georgie sat down and called. You can make the greatest list in the world, but nothing happens until you're in action; until you make the calls.

Which brings us to our next chapter, The Power Hour. Together with the Power 100, these two Activators can change your business.

[summary]

- Your Power 100 holds a key to your growth and success.
- Build a list of 100 people and companies who can and should work with you in five categories: direct prospects, referrals, indirect prospects, joint ventures and wish list.
- Organize the Power 100 into A, B, C, and W based on how "warm" they are to your services already.

- Gather the additional information you need to contact them successfully: what do they need, who at the company might be good to start with, and how do you contact them?
- Get ready to contact them—that's the next chapter.

[exercises]

1. Create your Power 100 List.

2. Gather the additional information you need to contact them.

3. Create a method you will use to manage the list, who you call, their response and your next steps.

The Power Hour
THE POWER TO TRANSFORM YOUR BUSINESS

Action. *Every business needs it, and most don't do enough of it—at least not planned action. The Power Hour creates precisely that: at least one hour every day of planned action.*

You've created your Power 100 based on the work you just did in the last chapter. Now you'll put that Power to work through The Power Hour, a non-negotiable date you make with yourself and the phone *every day*. We've watched businesses completely transform themselves by creating their Power 100 and coupling it with The Power Hour.

At first you are calling simply to connect, build relationships, explore what's happening in their world, make appointments, and provide

YOUR POWER HOUR MEANS YOU WILL PICK UP THE PHONE AND CALL THE PROSPECTS YOU IDENTIFIED IN THE POWER 100.

advice. You call to learn more about them, share ideas, and recommend ways that your products and services can solve their problems.

Then with connections established, you'll have knowledge of their needs and opportunities to propose your services.

Think of your Power Hour call like dating. You have to start with a cup of coffee and then a movie before you can ask them to marry you! Otherwise, they will be running for the hills.

NON-NEGOTIABLE

What in your life is non-negotiable?

Well, hopefully, paying your taxes stands towards the top of that list.

THE POWER HOUR IS NON-NEGOTIABLE BECAUSE IT IS CRITICALLY IMPORTANT TO YOUR BUSINESS.

Taking care of traffic tickets, getting your child to a doctor's appointment, brushing your teeth, maybe going to church each week. Whatever your answer, you already have non-negotiable appointments in your life. You've got non-negotiables because you know you'll get in some hot water if you don't or they are critically important to you and your family.

The Power Hour becomes your non-negotiable pact between you and your business. Non-negotiable means no excuse keeps you from executing, no excuse stops you from picking up the phone to call your prospects and friends who refer.

Non-negotiable doesn't mean when you feel like it. It doesn't mean when you have time. It doesn't mean after the 28 other things on your To-Do list. It doesn't mean "something more important came up so maybe tomorrow." Non-negotiable means it happens no matter what. Like getting the car repaired when it starts billowing black smoke. Like getting yourself to the doctor if you're sick. Your Power Hour is something that happens *no matter what.*

ON THE CALENDAR

The very best way to make sure your Power Hour happens every day means it goes on your calendar—just like your other critical appointments.

Depending on how best you work, you can place The Power Hour on the calendar at the same time every day to get into a great habit. Or you can vary the times throughout the week if you discover your customers are reachable at different times—and you have the discipline to fluctuate the time throughout your work day.

Placing The Power Hour on the calendar means the odds of doing these tasks increase. You significantly reduce the chances of leaving it to "whenever." You know how "whenever" operates: sometimes it arrives, sometimes it doesn't. "Whenever" does not equal non-negotiable.

Yes, lots of reasons crop up that seem to trump non-negotiable. When they do—and they will—look yourself in the mirror and say out loud

> *"This is the heart of my marketing.*
> *If I do this, I will succeed."*

Trust us; you will.

ONE MAGICAL HOUR

Once you start to see the results, you're going to love The Power Hour. The key rests in how you use it. The Power Hour represents your time on the phone calling prospects, friends who refer and former customers. It isn't time to research who you should call or practice what you're going to say. It isn't time to rearrange the papers on your desk or call a friend for moral support.

The Power Hour supplies you at least one solid hour on the phone. All your prep and practice happens before you get to The Power Hour. Now you're making the best use of every single minute in your hour.

When we say The Power Hour, we don't literally mean one hour. No rule exists that says your Power Hour couldn't be two or three hours every day. Once you get started and see the results, you'll want to keep this train moving at full speed. Start with an hour, at least, and build time as your calls get stronger and you begin to see the results.

If you need some targets, try our 10-2-5 guideline:

- **Make 10 calls every day.** Certainly you'll be leaving messages occasionally, but ten calls every day to start will get you on your path to success and some prospects will be home to accept your call.

- **Set 2 appointments every day.** Those appointments might be for the next phone call, a cup of coffee, or an in-house visit. When you initially reach your prospect, she might not have the flexibility to talk to you for any length of time. Share the reason for your call, who you are and why the benefits you bring might be valuable to her. Set the "real" appointment at a time when she can focus on a more in-depth conversation.

- **Get 5 new referrals every day.** In addition to using your calls to open conversations, set appointments and, of course, actually sell something, acquiring new prospects through referrals keeps your Power 100 growing. Who might your prospect know that you should be talking to, besides them?

The idea of calling intimidates many of us. If you've never made prospect calls before, map out a brief script to open the call and practice before you first pick up the phone. Then practice your opening until it feels and sounds natural. Brush your teeth and practice. Practice on your family at the dinner table. Put down your script and walk through your thoughts with a friend. Whatever you do, don't read your script when you call! Get comfortable with what you want to say, and the person on the other end will become comfortable with you.

Your first call, maybe first several calls, isn't to sell something. You want to create rapport with the prospect. If this is a completely cold call, you'll introduce yourself, share how you learned of the person or company and offer a little bit about why you called. Let's be honest—have you ever bought something from someone you didn't know who called out of the blue? Highly unlikely. Keep that in mind as you make your cold colds. Instead, develop rapport with the prospect. When you have, then set up an appointment to either meet them in-person or have a more in-depth call about what you can do for them. Think benefits first, service features second.

If this is a warm prospect you are calling—someone you know at least a little or has been referred to you—you still want to use this first call to introduce yourself, develop rapport and learn a little about the prospect. Ask them questions that open them up to sharing information with you. Remember those "what," "where," "how" and "when" questions we were taught when we were younger. Use them here to encourage a conversation. Again, your goal remains to set up a more extended in-person or phone conversation to really dig into the prospect's need and how you solve it.

THE FEAR OF CALLING

We know some of you struggle with picking up the phone. The idea of reaching out to someone that you don't know causes "YIKES!!!" and all kinds of nasty, queasy, avoidance techniques. Yet The Power Hour is non-negotiable, so that means you have to do it to be in business.

While 100 is the target number, we're taking away all excuses why you can't do this. Start with your Really, Really Powerful 20, those people who have already or can refer business to you. We love referrals—as you'll see in the Referral Chapter. One of our customers laser focused her Power Hour on her referrals and doubled the size of her business in one year. If you're fighting yourself about The Power Hour, start with people you know.

- Your success can be driven fast by the people who are willing to refer you, put you in front of your ideal customers or endorse you. You need to keep these people top of mind. Highlight your referral candidates on your Power 100 list. Keep this list by your side to ensure that you're thinking of them. When you do, you'll begin to notice opportunities to connect with them and get to know them.

- The Really, Really Powerful 20 gives you a large enough number to keep your focus expansive but narrow enough that you won't be overwhelmed.

- Call the person at the top of your list and when you've reached out to them, move them to the bottom of your list.

- Next, call the person who was Number 2 on The Really, Really Powerful 20 list (who is now Number 1 because you moved the first person down). Then move Number 2 and call Number 3. Shortly, you'll be back to your original Number 1. Call them again. Rotate. Rinse and repeat. Your Really, Really Powerful 20 list never dies.

- Call one Really, Really Powerful 20 person each day. Call them again in another 20 days. Stay in touch. Offer them articles you found that apply to them. Give them a tip on someone who could do business with them. Figure out how to cross-market and make them a business buddy (we'll share more in Chapter Partner Up).

- Now expand and do your Power 100 list. It gets easier once you've started and have some results.

- With a target of 10-2-5—ten calls a day; two appointments a day and five new referrals a day—your Power 100 not only never grows old, it keeps getting bigger!

At this moment, you might not think you can fill out your Really, Really Powerful 20. You can. Now that you know what you need to do, you'll start to take notice of the people you should add to this list.

People buy from people they trust, and trust isn't developed in one call. Depending on what you offer, you might need to "touch" the prospect through follow-up calls, e-mails, or in-person visits. You might need to "touch" them six to twelve times before they make a buying decision. While this might be slower than you'd like, wouldn't you be willing to put in that effort for a new customer?

WHILE THIS ISN'T A CHAPTER ABOUT SALES, LET'S FACE THE FACTS: THE POWER HOUR MEANS SELLING, RELATIONSHIP SELLING.

COMMIT AND REAP

When you commit to your daily Power Hour, the results you'll produce in a short period of time are so exciting and often so dramatic that the process becomes self-motivating. It's inspiring to connect with others, develop closer relationships and be able to provide solutions. What if this became your favorite part of the day? When you have something important to share, your call is not a bother. You're helping them as they help you.

Consider some real examples from our own business. Jennifer committed to The Power Hour, five days a week. In three months time, she *tripled* her revenue. Another customer increased his revenue by $79,000 in the first month of committing to his daily Power Hour. His revenue went up an additional $64,000 on top of that the second month. In the third month of The Power Hour, it went up an additional $52,000 on top of that.

We were curious why the number went down slightly between the second and third month. He confessed. He stopped doing his Power Hour consistently. When he got back on board again, he decided to hire three people to do the calls for him. He realized two things. First, The Power Hour totally worked, and he was making good money again. And, second, he didn't like making the calls, but he now had the funds to hire qualified sales people who were talented at calling. His results went back up and his business is thriving.

Perhaps our favorite story comes from Mary. She committed to doing her Power Hour daily. When her first day arrived, Mary wasn't ready to make her calls. Instead of doing something else, she chose to sit. Just sit. She sat still for one hour as her "penalty" for not being prepared and to teach herself it's more valuable to use the hour as its intended rather than suffer the sentence of just sitting. We love this story because Mary knew she had to get creative to manage herself and her non-negotiable pact with her business. Please feel free to borrow this idea from Mary if you find yourself in need of a push to step up to your Power Hour.

At this stage, the only difference between all of these customers and you rests on the fact that they made the calls and you are just starting. They did nothing that you can't do. Get prepared, practice before you call and then make the calls to your Power 100.

TRACK YOUR RESULTS

Now that you're rolling, what are your results? Obviously, you should track sales. Hey, why not *celebrate* sales? Make the event memorable and fun so you'll want to do it again and again. Other things need to be tracked, too, so you can make refinements and improve.

What you measure gets managed. Measuring the results of your calls fine-tunes The Power Hour. Here are some ideas of what you should be tracking.

- At what time of day do the most prospects answer the phone?
- What do you say that really catches people's interest?
- How many times are you calling or meeting with a prospect before they become interested?
- Do your phone calls or in-person meetings enable you to connect faster?
- How many great prospects—people really interested in working with you—turn into customers?

What else do you need to track for your business?

Track Your Power Hour

NAME	PHONE	WHAT YOU WANT THEM TO DO	WHEN YOU'LL CONTACT THEM

You'll find this and all the worksheets and examples for you to download at www.wideawakemarketing.com/resources

The more you know, the more refined and accurate your information, the better your calls will become. The better the calls, the better your results.

Many find they get the best results from their Power Hour by scheduling every day at the same time. Put it in your calendar just like you would any other non-negotiable appointment. It's only an hour out of your day, considerably less time than most people spend watching television.

TOUGH LOVE

We humans are funny beings. Sometimes our will to excel is bested by our fear of calling. If you're still finding it difficult to motivate yourself to do your Power Hour, find someone to whom you can be accountable.

Cultivate a work or personal friend who is willing to be your accountability partner. Tell them what your goals are—how much time you'll spend on your Power Hour each day, how many calls you want to make, how soon you'll make the next call, how often you ask for the sale. Then ask them to hold you by checking in daily to report on your actions. At the end of the week measure your actions against your goals and share that with them, too.

IF YOU ARE HAVING A HARD TIME BEING ACCOUNTABLE TO YOURSELF, BE ACCOUNTABLE TO SOMEONE ELSE.

Your accountability partner needs to check in very briefly with you every day if you miss contacting them. Tough love brings action.

RED, GREEN, YELLOW

Just like any other important meeting, The Power Hour requires uninterrupted time. If you work in an office, close your door and let your staff know that you're not to be disturbed.

Many of us work from home, and that comes with built-in distractions, things that can interrupt or sideline your Power Hour. For some that distraction might be the refrigerator calling you. For others, your children or spouse might be the interruption culprits.

A customer of ours created a genius system to manage the distractions built into her life. She devised a color card system for her family to use. When she was in her office, door closed, doing her Power Hour and her family needed her, she taught them to slip a colored card under the door. A green card meant that someone needed to talk to her. It wasn't urgent, but they needed her. She would check in with her family just as soon as she finished her Power Hour. A yellow card slid under the door meant they had something really important and needed to share it soon. She would address the issue when her current call was complete. A red card under the door meant, "Urgent." NOW! She would get off the phone as soon as possible to address the issue—and there had better be blood!

Train Your Family and Staff

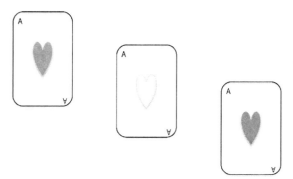

Her family eventually learned the system and used the green, yellow and red cards accurately. Frankly, this system works in office environments just as well as at home. The requirements for using each colored card might change—hopefully, no blood is spilled in your office—but the idea remains the same. Do not interrupt your Power Hour.

This is just one possibility for managing the distractions in your life that turn your attention away from the best, most productive hour of your day. Figure out a system that works for you and request the support you want from others to make your Power Hour successful.

REFRAME YOUR RESULTS

Several months ago we got a call from a business colleague, Bill. We talk periodically as he is one of our referral candidates, and we are one for him, also. Bill started whining on this particular call. He just spent the past several months working with ten prospects and only one became his customer. Bill felt he had wasted a lot of time to only land one new customer. This seemed to be his average—ten good prospects would turn into one great customer. He wanted to figure out how to improve his results.

"Bill, let's reframe your results," we said.

Bill travels in the high-end atmosphere of expensive consultants which explains his answer to our next question. We asked him what the monetary value of his one sale was worth. $30,000 he said.

Here comes the reframe. Are you ready? It's powerful and applies to you, not just Bill. One sale netted Bill $30,000. But he couldn't make that one sale if he hadn't done the ten calls. Every one of those ten calls earned him $3,000.

You need to measure the results of your Power Hour the same way. You must recognize that every call should be made to find your best customer candidate. Without all the calls and visits, no new customer will materialize. Customers just don't stop by and knock on your office door.

What's your math? How many great prospects do you talk to in order to create one great customer?

Consider the following metrics. Let's say that out of 100 calls or handshakes, you have 40 meaningful conversations. Let's say that out of

40 conversations, you create ten sales. If one sale equals $500, then ten sales equal $5,000. That means every call you make actually puts $50 in your pocket! You had to make those 100 calls or handshakes to create the ten sales. Without the 100 calls or handshakes there would be no ten sales. Figure out the equation for your business, and remember it the next time you want to skip the networking event or not make your Power Hour calls. Put it on a piece of paper and prominently display it where you work and will see it every day.

Example:

100 calls or handshakes = 40 conversations

40 conversations = 10 sales

1 sale = $500

10 sales = $5000

EACH CALL = $50

You:

_____ Calls or handshakes =_____ conversations

_____ Conversations =_____ sales

_____ Sale = $_____

_____ Sales = $_____

Each Call = $_____

Once you experience the joy of connecting with your potential customers and you start to feel the momentum of increased referrals and business, excitement quickly replaces nervousness.

If you feel that little shiver of anxiousness as you pick up the phone or walk into an office, remind yourself of the value you have to offer others. You bring them solutions to their problems and answers to their needs. When you express genuine interest in them and be your true, authentic self, good things happen. Establish trust. Trust happens person-to-person, one relationship at a time.

If you're feeling challenged about making your calls, it may also help to get clear about the value of each call to your business. We know, after coaching hundreds of business owners, that the Power Hour is literally the make-or-break hour of your day. No kidding.

CALL AND GROW

Your Power Hour is, hands down, the most significant customer activation step you can implement if you're serious about increasing your business. Make it a priority. Make it fun. Make it real. But most of all, make it happen. As a business owner, this is the most powerful hour of your day.

[summary]

- Your Power Hour is non-negotiable. Do it at least one hour every day.
- Your goal initially is to build rapport with the prospect, not leap in and start selling.
- Your targets should be 10-2-5: ten calls, two appointments and five new referrals every day.
- Practice, practice, practice before you call so you're confident and natural.
- If you're having a hard time motivating yourself, get an Accountability Partner.
- Track your results.
- Determine the value of each phone call.

[exercises]

1. Draft a script to help you open your calls. Practice it out loud. Practice with friends or family.

2. Develop a simple method of tracking your results against your weekly objectives. Include:

   a. How many calls you made in each of the four Power 100 List categories _____

   _____

   _____

   _____

   b. What are your objectives for this week's calls? _____

   _____

   _____

   _____

   c. What did you actually achieve versus your objectives? _____

   _____

   _____

   _____

   d. How many great prospects become customers? _____

   _____

   _____

   _____

e. What is the value of each of your conversations/handshakes?

_____

_____

_____

The Referral System

CULTIVATE YOUR MOST VALUABLE ASSETS

Referrals. *Everyone loves them. Think about it. Your highly satisfied customer is so excited about the experience they've had with you that they rave about you to their colleagues, give them your number and urge them to call you so they too can experience all the benefits of working with you. What's not to love?*

REFERRALS ARE GOLD

Whenever we teach a marketing seminar, we ask "Who among you gets some of your business from referrals?" Every hand goes up in the room. Then we ask the kicker. "How many of you get *all* your business from referrals?" Stunningly, most of the hands stay up.

Are you stunned that we say stunned?

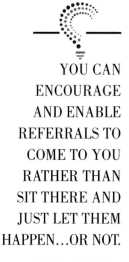

YOU CAN
ENCOURAGE
AND ENABLE
REFERRALS TO
COME TO YOU
RATHER THAN
SIT THERE AND
JUST LET THEM
HAPPEN...OR NOT.

Yes, we love referrals, too. But you can't just let them happen to you...or not. You see our third question is then "How many of you encourage referrals?" Almost every hand goes down.

So let me get this straight. You love referrals. You get all or much of your business from referrals. Yet you do nothing to encourage referrals. That feels like playing with fire to us.

What if one day those referrals that just happen to you stop coming in for whatever reason? What if what you took for granted goes away? You'll have no business or one that is severely damaged. But unbeknownst to lots of people it seems.

WHY WE LOVE REFERRALS— AND THEY LOVE YOU

We love referrals for many reasons. First of all, a referral already knows something about you. They've already heard enough about your products or services to pique their interest so you don't have to spend as much time explaining or getting them "up to speed." In the mind of the person referred, you already have "expert" status, preeminence—a very valuable place to begin a relationship. It means you can focus faster on connecting with the referral to determine their need, rather than having to establish your credibility.

Trust, such a key component in making a sale, has already taken its first steps. That's because the referrer—the friend or colleague who told them about you—had a good experience and recommends you. Much of the research and evaluation of you has already been done by the referring person. It's a shortcut for the prospect to quickly and efficiently get to "Yes."

We also love referrals because they're predisposed to purchase. The referred prospect is already either part way or all the way sold on your business. They've already heard the benefits of working with you and are interested enough to contact you (or take your call).

The referred prospect also typically drops into your Product Funnel at a deeper level. Remember that the top of your Product Funnel contains your no-to-low cost offerings because it removes risk and begins establishing a relationship. A good referral, delightfully, usually bypasses those introductory levels. They already know you "through" the person who referred them. That means they often buy more expensive, or more advanced, products and services sooner. With trust already established, they are less sensitive to price than a cooler lead.

WHO ARE YOUR WALKING EVANGELISTS?

With referrals being so valuable, so golden, wouldn't you think that we would pay close attention to creating and nurturing them? To stop waiting for them to fall out of the sky and into our laps? And when a referral does show up, that we would have a system of some sort in place to track who sent them to us and what the outcome of the call was?

Asking for and encouraging referrals will get you much farther than waiting for the planets to align and drop them in your lap. Referrals happen because we humans like to help others. When you've had a customer who has had a wonderful experience, they know and trust you. They often want the opportunity to help someone else get the same benefits.

A STRONG REFERRAL SYSTEM HELPS YOU RECOGNIZE JUST WHO YOUR PRIMARY REFERRING FRIENDS ARE AND SIMPLIFIES ENCOURAGING YOUR WALKING EVANGELISTS.

John used the Power 100 to create a list of former patients and friends who could (or already had) referred business to him. He made it a practice to ask his patients for referrals. He put signs up in all his patient rooms sharing that he would be "honored" if they referred. He put a simple worksheet by the phone, and the receptionist asked every new caller how they had heard about Dr. John. Because John did the work to increase referrals instead of waiting for them to just happen, his practice grew. But you knew that already, didn't you? So here's a little more detail about what success looked like to John. He was able to bring in another dentist to take some of his work so John could concentrate on other aspects of his business. His win: more revenue, more happy patients, and less time at work for John.

Your Walking Evangelists might not just be former or current customers. They might be colleagues who complement what you do. They might be colleagues or friends who are natural connectors. They might be association presidents. They might even be family or friends who are completely convinced you do great work. Frankly, it could be just about anybody.

So your first step is to figure out who is *already* referring business to you, and then determine who *can* refer business. Make a vow to never "just" let referrals happen to you. Make them happen.

WHEN'S THE BEST TIME TO ASK?

Most business owners who do ask for referrals wait to ask when their customers have been with them for a while and have had some experience with their product or service. Although this may seem logical, it's not actually the best time to ask for the referral.

The best time to ask is when they first say "yes" to the purchase. This is when your new customer is most excited about what you have to offer, about your potential to solve his problem or meet his need. He's at the highest emotional peak. He feels relieved to finally have an answer. He believes that you will solve his problem. He's most hopeful and filled with anticipation.

He's also fresh off the evaluation cycle. He has asked the questions and you've successfully dealt with his objections. He's educated about the purchase. He's best prepared to answer questions that a new prospect might have and support that newcomer through any resistance because he has just gone through that process himself.

It's true that later on he might have more information, but that doesn't necessarily work in your favor. Having more data often clouds opinions. With more experience comes more room for complexity and judgment that may complicate the information we share with others.

THE MOST OPPORTUNE MOMENT IS WHEN THE PROSPECT SAYS "YES" TO THE PURCHASE AND BECOMES A CUSTOMER.

The Art of The Ask

Have you ever felt like you've been "hit up" for a referral? It didn't feel good, did it? Didn't encourage you to provide one. Have you ever been asked "Who could you refer to me?" and notice that your brain shuts down, cramps up. You might have known before they asked, but now that you've been asked... It's like asking your child "How was school today?" You don't get much of an answer.

So, yes, there is an art to asking for referrals. When you hit someone with a direct question such as, "Do you have anyone else that you could refer to me?" you get you the blank stare. It's not that they don't want to give you a referral, but the question can land as confrontational or simply shuts the mind down. You've probably had this experience yourself. You feel "put on the spot" for a response, and your mind goes blank. The question also doesn't engage the person you're asking because it's all about you and what you want—there's not much in it for them.

Next time try inquiring about a referral this way:

"If you know others who may benefit from our services like you have, we'd be honored by your referrals."

By invoking the idea of honor, you *bestow something back to the giver.* They get to feel like they're doing something beneficial for the person they're referring, plus they're giving you a compliment through their confidence in you.

Make your appreciation for referrals obvious. A chiropractor we worked with several years ago made a poster for each of his patient rooms with this message: "We know that you'll feel great when your friends and family feel great. You can give something every special to those you care about—the same relief from pain that you've received from us. We are honored to take care of those that you refer to us."

Plus they gave the referring patient a 30-minute complimentary massage as a thank you gift for any referral who becomes a patient.

Does the system generate a steady stream of qualified referrals for the office? All evidence says "YES." The referring patients feel great about helping those they care about get out of pain; they have the prestige of being the one to link the doctor to the person in need; and they are appreciated with a gift for doing so. It's a win-win-win.

CREATE YOUR REFERRAL SYSTEM

How do you begin? Go to your Power 100 list and find those who have already referred prospects to you or those that would be good candidates to do so. Also ask your customers. Now you need to gather and keep that information someplace other than your head.

Simple Referral System Excel Spreadsheets

Date	Prospect	Referred By	Service	Status	Thank You
8/25	Mary Smith	Ed Jones	Massage	Booked 1st Appt	Sent 8/26
9/3	Jim Evers	Linda Carlisle	Adjustment	1st Call Complete	Sent 9/4
9/5	ABC Company	Ed Jones	Bi-weekly Staff Massage	1st Call Complete	Sent 9/6
9/12	Marile Edwards	Vivian Larsen	Pain Relief	Booked	Sent 9/13

You'll find this and all the worksheets and examples for you to download at www.wideawakemarketing.com/resources

You must develop a system for tracking where your leads come from. You can do this in a spreadsheet or a contact management program (CRM, or Customer Relationship Management programs). You want to gather:

- The name of the prospect calling you
- Their contact information
- Their need…and the contents of your conversation (you'll have more than one)
- The name of the person who referred them

Now you have an official record of who your Walking Evangelists are, who has been helping you build your business—without your encouragement. Treat them well. They are busy spreading the word of Y-O-U.

Show your appreciation by thanking them for their referral. Call them, send them a handwritten note, and maybe mail them a gift. Think of a gift that would be meaningful for them and is commensurate with the value of the lead. Can you send pizza to their office, or perhaps a fresh bouquet of flowers? Making a charitable donation in their name is almost always appropriate and appreciated.

TRAIN YOUR EVANGELISTS

You've already put your very best referral sources on your Power 100 List because they have the power to change your business. That's because Walking Evangelists are almost like a little mini-sales force. Would you send a sales force out to sell your services without some training? No, of course not.

So you want to train these ambassadors. They need to know the kinds of customers you're looking for, the Ideal Prospects for your business. They should understand the nature of the product your Ideal Prospect is trying to solve. Your Evangelists need a little bit of information about what you offer and the benefits your customers receive when they work with you. Perhaps you even give them your brochure, business cards or other support information they might need to make it easy for them to continue sending prospects your way.

Now the ball is back in your court. Above all else, please make sure you contact every prospect you receive, no matter whether you think they are a fit or not. Make a promise to those that refer to you that you will *always* call and follow up. You want to make them look good and demonstrate that you can be trusted to take their referrals seriously and handle them professionally.

If you step up to actively encouraging referrals, instead of them just happening to you, you will change your business. The trick is to know who your wonderful, thoughtful, kind, encouraging Evangelists are and can be. Treat them well, treat their referrals well, systematize your referral process and success is yours.

[summary]

- Referrals "just happen" to most businesses.
- Referrals are some of the best prospects you will ever have.
- You should be encouraging and creating referrals, not just waiting for them to happen to you.
- The best time to ask for a referral is the moment a customer buys from you.
- Determine who your Walking Evangelists already are.
- Add to that group those who can refer business to you.
- Perfect how you ask for referrals in ways that honor the Walking Evangelist.
- Your Walking Evangelists need training to bring you the "right" customer for your services.
- A simple Referral system will enable you to track not only who is referred but who refers, and permits you to say "thank you."
- Always, always, always call prospects who are referred to you, even if you think they aren't appropriate for your business.
- Send a "thank you" note and small gift, if possible, to the person who refers. They will remember you and refer again.

[exercises]

1. Create three different ways of asking for referrals that "honor" the person referring. Track which one works best and use it.

2. Develop a simple, written method of tracking your referrals each week. Include:

a. How many referrals were "just" received and from whom? _____

_____

_____

_____

b. How many Walking Evangelists did you train or speak with? ____

_____

_____

_____

c. Who is referring the most prospects to you?

_____

_____

_____

d. What did you actually achieve versus your objectives? _____

_____

_____

_____

e. How many great referrals become customers? _____

_____

_____

_____

Reviving the Dead
MINE THE GOLD
YOU ALREADY HAVE

Customers. *They are the end goal, the Holy Grail, the prize in the Cracker Jack. If you've been in business for any length of time—five years, five decades or five minutes—and you have former customers, you have a great, unappreciated asset to help your business grow.*

For those of you already in business, this Activator is Gold. Your former customers provide the avenue to new business because here's the truth:

They're not actually dead. They're just sleeping, most likely because you haven't been talking to them.

These are former customers who once did business with you but aren't today. Generally, there are exceptional reasons why they aren't doing business with you today.

109

- They don't know you "do that." How many times have you checked in on a former customer to see how she's doing only to hear that she just bought something you offer from someone else. When you point out that you could have provided that service, she replies, "I didn't know you did that." That's like a knife through your Income Statement. That statement alone should convince you to stay in touch with former customers.

- They don't know what you've added. Perhaps the last time you worked with this customer, you were missing the follow-on product she needed. But your Product Funnel is probably more mature and expansive now. Do your former customers know that? Probably not.

- They don't know you as a leader. Perhaps you weren't clear about your Preeminence and abdicated your role as expert so former customers saw no one to guide them to the next step.

- They might have a problem. Maybe you're a little afraid to call them. What if they didn't like the product or service you delivered? Well, calling them enables you to find out and if there's a problem, fix it. They just might return to you because you were willing to fix what didn't happen.

- They might have slipped your mind. Perhaps you just got so focused on generating new leads and closing new business that you neglected the folks who already love you and have proven their loyalty to you in the past.

There might be other reasons, but I bet you see where this is going. Your former customers need to hear from you. Who knows how much business is bundled up inside them, waiting to find the right business to provide the service? That business should be yours.

If they chose you once, it's highly likely that they're predisposed to work with you again. Rather than chasing stone-cold leads, why not make your life easier and work with the warm leads you've already got?

WORK WITH WHO BROUGHT YOU

What a simple idea. Reviving your former customers. It seems so simple that you're probably bopping yourself on the head right now saying, "I knew that!" We know. We see it over and over again.

This story should make you weep… and then hopefully, call some former customers.

One of our customers has a hearing aid store with a database of 3,500 people who have bought from him in the past. We asked him how often a person needs to buy a new hearing aide. He said about once every three years. We asked him about how many former customers in his database had purchased hearing aids over three years ago. He estimated about two-thirds. We asked what he was doing with that database, and he said, "Nothing." So we challenged him to start making calls to all those people who already liked him and had purchased from him in the past. He scheduled 17 new appointments in the first week alone. One month into his outreach, he'd increased revenue in his practice by an additional $79,000! His customers were thrilled to hear from him (no pun intended), and they appreciated the opportunity to upgrade their hearing aid products to ones that served them better.

He had $79,000 sitting in his database, and that's just one month's worth of effort. Can you imagine how much business is sitting in his entire database of former customers? Can you imagine how much business is sitting in *your* entire database of former customers?

Well, let's find out.

RELATIONSHIP, RELATIONSHIP, RELATIONSHIP

Ready to start making some calls to former customers? These are not "Hi, would you like to buy a pound of whatever-I-am-selling?" calls. When making calls to revive your former customers, your primary intention is to *serve* them not *sell* them. If it's been a while since you've contacted them, the purpose of your call is to check in, see how they're doing, find out what's happening for them first so you can better know how to serve them. They haven't exactly been waiting around for your call. They might even feel abandoned or a little cranky that they haven't heard from you.

Practice patience with this Reviving The Dead process and focus on relationship building. While every industry is different, most businesses report that 80 percent of their customers purchase between the fifth and seventh interaction.

Your job is to be patient.

Ask the right questions about your prospect's business and next steps every time you "touch" him with a call, a message or a communication. You're just that much closer to a sale.

SIX WAYS TO REVIVE THE DEAD

If you're scratching you heads about how to begin your Revive the Dead outreach, here are some action steps to follow.

1. **Set your intention and have a plan.** Calling up a former customer you haven't talked to in months (or years) and pitching them on your latest product will likely sound a bit mercenary. Think of how you would respond to such a call. You risk losing a very good prospect. Focus instead on reestablishing contact with

them first. Have a long-range plan that includes the intention of turning them into an active customer again but remember not to become so focused on the goal that you lose touch with nurturing the relationship. And on the other hand, don't spend so much time nurturing the relationship that you forget your goal is to revive them.

2. **Be prepared.** Refresh your knowledge about this person before you pick up the phone to call them. What did they buy from you and when? What was their experience like? What problems did you solve for them? What was their most likely next step based on the work you did with them last? Do you recall anything personal or unique about them (names of their children or spouse, their hobbies or interests)? Set your purpose and course in your mind before you call, e-mail or contact them.

3. **Reestablish yourself as an expert.** Look for opportunities to share your expertise, particularly if they "didn't know you did that." Look for a way to give something back to them and reestablish the benefits of working with you. Focus on their problem or need. Talk about that and what it would be like to have that problem solved or need delivered. *Do not solve their problem when you talk to them.* If you solve their problem, they don't need to work with you, do they?

4. **Give them something free.** Everyone loves getting something for free. It's a tactic we frequently use in getting new customers but one we forget to use with existing customers. Offer a free e-book, your instructional newsletter, a report, or something of value that will remind them of the benefits of working with you.

5. **Express your appreciation**. Take the time to tell them you appreciated working with them and appreciated their business. Give them some love. Most of us suffer from chronic under-appreciation. A genuine expression of gratitude goes a very long way, because it's so rare in the business world. When was the last time someone thanked you for your business? It's been awhile, hasn't it? Yet I'm sure you love it when it does happen. Think of ways to thank your customers. Take a group of them to lunch and ask them to invite their business friends who might need your services. Create customer appreciation and loyalty programs that give special benefits and rewards to your best customers. These are just a few ideas. What are yours?

6. **Ask for a Success Story.** You've probably thought of Success Stories as a way to build your credibility because they're more powerful than simple testimonials. Your instincts on that are right on the money. Now we want you to recognize another power that Success Stories bring: a way to acknowledge and honor your customers. By highlighting a customer with his name, company name or photo and allowing him to share his experience, you honor him as a spokesperson for you and give them a chance to "show off" his own success. While many larger businesses resist participating in Success Stories because they seem more beneficial to you than them, don't give up too easily. If you cast the business as a hero, they get a completely different benefit than they've received from a Success Story before. They get time in the spotlight, can showcase how great their business is, and show how always-current they are keeping their business as an "expert."

We prefer Success Stories to testimonials, which too often provide only the obvious: "I loved Mary and you should work with her, too!" That doesn't tell your prospect anything.

A Success Story is tightly focused: a short, three-part, three-sentence discussion of the work you did with the customer. A well-written Success Story allows your prospects to see themselves in the story, understand your expertise in addressing their need and vicariously experience the results they can expect in working with you.

The three sentences of a Success Story are:

1. The Problem or Need your customer was facing before working with you. Only if you have permission to use the story can you identify the customer by name. Obtaining permission will probably hang on whether you can reveal the problem in a way that doesn't embarrass your customer, a way that makes your customer a hero, not a victim.

2. The Solution you provided to resolve the problem or need.

3. The Results, benefits or outcomes the customer received through working with you. The more you can quantify and provide hard benefits the better. Soft benefits are fine, but not as powerful as results they can see and count!

Want an example?

"A Senior Manager in a critical role with deep but narrow experience was preparing to leave our client company due to perceived limited career opportunities. We coupled our assessment program and unique methodology with coaching to identify leadership strengths and potential derailers. The result: the Senior Manager was retained and transitioned into a bigger general management role, and the company saved $200,000 in external recruitment costs.

Need. Solution. Result.

READY TO REVIVE

If you've got former customers, it's time to revive them. First, look at your existing database and highlight who you should add to your "A" list of contacts in your Power 100. Start with the people you feel most comfortable contacting, the ones most receptive to you and most likely to feel excited about reconnecting with you. Now you've got some results to propel your momentum and excitement for this Activator. Now you're ready to divide the list into your "B" and "C" categories to contact them in the same manner.

Next, write down some goals and create a plan for yourself. How many contacts do you have on your Revive the Dead list? How many people will you call every day? How many days a week? How long will it take you to move through your list? What time of the day will you block off for your calls? What kind of support will you put in place to keep you accountable and inspired? Make sure each of your former customers is a part of your Power 100 to insure you make the outreach.

Next, review the strategies above and choose those that best serve you and your customers. Different customers will require different strategies. Customize your calls to meet your customer's preferences, not yours. Then just pick up the phone and dial.

PICK UP THE PHONE

Of all the methods for contacting your former customers—or any customers or prospects you've had some contact with, frankly—calling them on the phone is not only the most personal, it's the most effective and usually the most preferred way of reconnecting. Let's test this. Do you want another e-mail? Do you read the ones you get now? Okay. E-mails aren't the best to Revive the Dead. Do you see the promotions, letters and advertisements that come to your postal mailbox? Do you read them? Do you have the budget to send at least three cards in a very short period of time (because it takes at least three cards in a very close interval for someone to "see" just one of the cards)? Nope. So postcards and letters to their mailbox are off the list.

That leaves phone calls. We know some of you hate to call, but you have to put yourselves out there. Phone calls are "the" best way to reconnect, to Revive Your Dead. If it's the best way and it's practically free, why wouldn't you just pick up the phone and call? You might have to call several times to reach your former customers. The odds are superior they aren't avoiding your call. They are busy with their business, work and family. You're not in it. So don't think you're the reason. Odds are you aren't. Call at different times of the day. When you do talk to them, ask the best time to reach them. Put that information in your database. Now you'll know for the next time.

Reviving the Dead is such a powerful Activation tool because you are mining the gold that's right there under your feet, buried in your existing database. Once you get rolling and experience the joy and financial rewards of reconnecting with your customers, you'll wonder why you didn't do this sooner.

[summary]

- Former customers are one of the very richest resources you can tap to open new business opportunities.
- Start by rebuilding your relationship, not by selling.
- Create a plan of who to contact, how to reestablish your expertise, provide something for free, express your appreciation for their past business and ask for what's next.

- Ask for and write Success Stories to demonstrate the work you do and the results you achieve.
- Identify people in your database, prepare and call them.

[exercises]

1. How many former customers do you have? If 10 percent of them returned to do business with you, how much revenue would that deliver, assuming they spend as much as last time? What if 20 percent returned?

   _____

   _____

   _____

2. If ten percent of your former customers returned to work with you again and this time spent ten percent more money with you, how much revenue would that create? If they spent twenty percent more?

   _____

   _____

   _____

3. If both of the above happened, what percentage of your yearly revenue target would be achieved, easing the pressure to create new, more expensive prospects?

   _____

   _____

   _____

4. Write your first Success Story:

    The Problem: _____

    _____

    _____

    _____

    Your Solution: _____

    _____

    _____

    _____

    The Result: _____

    _____

    _____

    _____

Partner Up

CREATING LEVERAGING PARTNERSHIPS

Peanut butter and jelly. *Salty and sweet. Classic combinations create great and memorable partnerships. The greatest strengths of each combine to create something even better for both.*

A memorable partnership for you might create a similar success. Think Microsoft and NBC (MSNBC), Oprah and Dr. Phil (in the beginning), Jillian Michaels and "The Biggest Loser." Once you start looking, you'll see lots of examples of people who created better business for each other by teaming up.

The next Activation step in your Customer Generator System examines ways to partner up with others.

Here's a News Flash for you business owners who suffer from the "Lone Ranger" syndrome: **Stop it!**

DOING EVERYTHING BY YOURSELF ISN'T HEROIC. IT'S JUST SHORTSIGHTED.

For those of you with a new business, Partnering with an established business—one that has already earned the trust of your Ideal Customer *and* complements what you do—offers a swift start-up path. If you're established but have a small database, a Partnership with another company that's already developed a solid base in your target market gives you a direct path to that warm pool.

If you're given a choice—to start from scratch or build on the connections of an established business—which would you choose? Immediate access to tens, hundreds or thousands of Ideal Prospects is pretty tantalizing.

WHAT IS A PARTNERSHIP?

In the kind of Partnership we're talking about, you team up temporarily to another company, probably through a contract that lays out what you plan to do together. (You won't be starting a new business together; we're talking about marketing partnerships, not legal partnerships.) In marketing-style Partnerships, you're going to do certain work and your partner will do other, complementary work to generate new business or revenue for each of you.

An effective Partnership must be win-win for both parties; otherwise why would you or your prospective partner work together? When you consider what makes a good partner, you're looking for:

- An established business
- That already has customers
- Who perfectly fit the profile of your Ideal Customer
- And what that business does complements, not competes, with yours

Working with such a partner enables you to:

- Gain access to lots of new Ideal Prospects right away without searching for them one or two at a time

- Laser focus your marketing dollars or efforts in the most fertile places
- Make money by winning new business

That's your WIN. But just what is the WIN for the other business? Lots. They:

- Endear and embed themselves more solidly with their existing customers by offering them the "next" thing they need
- Reduce or eliminate competition from grabbing their customers (the more you buy from one source the less likely you are to leave)
- Make some money for doing nothing more than marketing to their customers. They don't have to create a new product or service or create any back-office support such as billing or customer service.

Here's how the right partnership can jumpstart growth. Stephanie runs an exercise boot camp and wanted to grow her business. She realized that there were at least two other business owners in the area who served her Ideal Customer, yet they didn't compete with Stephanie. She approached them to discuss how they might "share" their customers. The three decided to hold an open house and invite all of their customers to a complimentary evening of wine tasting. The night of the party the office was flowing with customers from all three businesses. Before the wine tasting started, each of the three introduced themselves and their business. They provided material about their services and made a special, extraordinary offer. The result: Stephanie doubled her clientele in only 90 days. Customers of the other two businesses found Stephanie. Plus the other two business owners attracted new customers.

Win-win-win.

Partnering up grew three businesses through one event. And of course, they've had other wine tastings and more results since. Never underestimate the power of wine!

FIVE REASONS TO PARTNER UP

Aside from freeing you from the Lone Ranger syndrome and potentially making your life much easier, here are five excellent reasons to partner up with other businesses:

1. **Grow your database.** By partnering with another company that offers complementary services to yours, you both tap into a readily available group of prospects. This means each of you have the opportunity to expand your databases with more good leads.

2. **Add to your product funnel.** By partnering with another company that provides complementary products and services, you increase the offerings that are available to your customers, as do they. Instead of five things to choose from, you might be able to offer them double or triple the options. By partnering with others, you still receive a percentage of the revenue, yet you bypass all the time and energy required to create a new product on your own.

3. **Opportunity to cross-sell.** Cross-selling means that you provide a product or service to your partner's customers, and they provide one to yours. You sell complementary products and services to each other's lists.

4. **Transfer respect.** Remember the expression, "Birds of a feather flock together." When you partner with someone who already has a well-known reputation, their credibility transfers to you. By aligning yourself with someone you and your Ideal Prospects already respect, you garner respect as well.

5. **Acquire expertise.** Partnerships also help you acquire new expertise. By innovating new products and services that would

benefit both parties, you'll likely gain more knowledge that will benefit your customers and your business.

HOW DO I CHOOSE A PARTNER?

To answer this question, let's start with some self-reflection. When you look at the list above, what grabs you as most important? What do you want to create from the Partnership? Which of the five benefits is your top priority? Know this before you start. Otherwise you may find yourself heading in the wrong direction with the wrong partner.

When you are clear about what you want, start searching for the company that would be a good partner. Look for a company that has the same target market as yours and offers products and services that complement, but don't compete, with you. You want a company that is open to partnering, willing to work with you, excited about creating new offerings and blending services. How could the partnership enhance both of your brands? Ask yourself: Who can help me grow my business? Who can help me fill a void? Who targets the same audience that I do?

If you have a massage business, seek out personal trainers as partners. If you offer health supplements, identify some chiropractors in your area who treat the whole person. Someone out there complements what you do. Go find them.

WHAT'S IN IT FOR THEM?

Once you've identified some good Partnership prospects, take the time to examine the proposition from their point of view. The strongest Partnerships create a significant wins for both parties. Before contacting them, you want to make sure that you have some good ideas about what you bring to the party. What do you have to offer? What products and services can you provide that would benefit their customers? What problems can you solve for them? What do they want that only your company can provide?

By doing some research, you'll start with at least an idea of what's important to them. Maybe they're launching a new division so they don't have a lot of products and services in their funnel yet. Perhaps you already have a well-established product that would fill the gap, or you have expertise to lend in that area.

Open your mind to think through the win-win possibilities before you approach the prospective partner.

When you show that you've thought it through—when you bring at least a strawman plan rather than just a raw idea—they'll be more confident that you can follow it through to success.

STRUCTURE A WINNING PARTNERSHIP

The goal of the Partnership is always win-win, and there are several ways to structure it. You may have heard of partnerships called joint ventures or affiliate relationships. We break down the possibilities a little more simply.

The most obvious structure is a "Two-Way" partnership. In this model, you and your partner construct a letter or e-mail to send to each other's customers. You have something to sell their database, and they have something to sell yours. You think it's likely that your customers want what your Partner has to sell, so rather than leaving them on their own to find it, you introduce it to them through a recommendation. You receive some kind of a "spiff" or percentage of the sales. Your customer gets what they want, your partner makes a sale, and you get compensation for introducing them. Your partner does the same for you.

You'll want to retain ownership (always!) of your own database and track the sales that happen as a result of the Partnership so you can evaluate its success. You might co-create a landing page (or a mini website) with a special URL address so you can track the promotion and the leads that result.

Databases—the goldmine of customer names and contact information—are a treasured, valuable, secure asset of any company, including yours as you grow. Respect the ownership of that asset.

If you are selling your products through their database, you write the e-mails or letter. They mail them. The e-mail can point them to a special website, as mentioned above, or a unique phone number so you *both* can track the success of the campaign.

Another option is a "One-Way" partnership. This is a good strategy for a new business that

Let me repeat a key point: NEVER GIVE YOUR DATABASE TO YOUR PARTNER, OR ANYONE ELSE FOR THAT MATTER. NEVER ASK YOUR PROSPECTIVE PARTNER FOR THEIR DATABASE. IT'S A GREAT WAY TO END A GOOD DISCUSSION RAPIDLY.

doesn't have a large database yet. The same guidelines apply as a "Two-Way" partnership. You find a company that already has your Ideal Customers, whose products and services complement yours. The partner markets your products and services into their database in exchange for a percentage of the sales. The partner also benefits by providing customers with added services to meet their needs, generating greater loyalty and satisfaction.

A third partnership model uses bonuses, gift certificates or coupons that are passed out to the customer. If you're a chiropractor for example, you might create a coupon for a discounted massage and ask the local health club you're partnering with to include that in their monthly statement to members. You give the health club a percentage of the sale, a fairly effortless way for them to generate additional revenue, plus it gives their members the "gift" of the discounted coupon, bonus or opportunity.

KEEP IT CLEAN

It's always a good idea to write down and document your Partnership agreement. Be clear up front about how you will dissolve the Partnership when it runs its course or doesn't work out. Make sure you understand and agree about who "owns" the leads and who has rights to the database names, particularly if you've developed products and services together. Get some advice about whether you need a legal contract or whether you can do it yourself with an on-line contract and a handshake.

DEFINING AGREEMENTS AT THE BEGINNING SETS YOU UP FOR A MORE SUCCESSFUL PARTNERSHIP IN THE LONG RUN.

Thinking about how you would dissolve the partnership doesn't mean you're being pessimistic. It means you're acting like an astute business owner.

Successful Partnerships have the power to dramatically and rapidly transform your business. Is this one of the best ways to take *your* business to the next level?

[summary]

- Partnerships build businesses quickly.
- The best partners are established, have already established a base of your Ideal Customers and offer services that are complementary, not competing, to yours.
- The benefits of building through a Partnership include growing your database, adding to your Product Funnel, extending

cross-selling opportunities, transferring respect and acquiring new expertise.

- Do your research on prospective partners to determine what's in it for them. Before you approach, create a draft plan. A plan, even the wrong one, is better than a raw idea as it gets the conversation pointed in the right direction and shows you did your homework.

- The three most common models for Partnerships are "Two-Way," where both parties approach their customers; "One-Way," where one party approaches its customers; and Bonuses/Certificates where one party offers something special to the other's customers.

- **Never** give out your database to a partner or ask a partner for theirs.

- Contract your Partnership and determine how you'll end it before you start.

[exercises]

1. Brainstorm ten companies that would make good partners for you:

_____

_____

_____

2. What would you offer them?

_____

_____

_____

3. What would you like them to offer you?

_____

_____

_____

4. Contractually, what *must* you have from this relationship? It's non-negotiable.

_____

_____

_____

Off-Line and On-Line Networking
MAKE A CONNECTION

New "friends." *This new world we live and market in demands that we are out meeting new people, talking, sharing and serving. The days of driving business in the comfort of your bunny slippers is a quaint idea, left over from years gone by. Networking is our path to profits these days. Whether you're networking on-line by blogging, Facebooking, Tweeting and posting videos, or networking off-line by heading off to live events, making new friends is the gateway to new prospects.*

But how narrow is that gate? Today too many businesses invest in social networking with no new prospects or customers to show for it. Others come home from live events with little more than a pocket full of business cards. It's not just about appearing or showing up.

Otherwise, as Betty White said on Saturday Night Live, "What a big old waste of time!"

IT'S ABOUT HAVING STRATEGIES THAT ATTRACT YOUR NEW CONNECTIONS BACK TO YOU, TO YOUR PHONE, YOUR WEBSITE, YOUR E-MAIL BOX.

When you understand not just how to post and blog but how to *convert* your readers and listeners to prospects, every ounce of your social networking effort will pay off. When you know precisely what to say at the networking event and what to do with all those business cards when you come home, your time becomes revenue-generating. New connections become new friends. New friends become new prospects. New prospects become new customers—whether you're networking on-line or off.

One of our customers is the poster child for networking. She makes it a part of her everyday activities and has for years. Hope is a master at networking, and several years ago that skill paid off a million times over. She was starting a new business and needed serious money to get rolling—venture capital and angel-investor-type money. Hope had a huge asset. She had been a natural networker her whole life. She made it a point to stay in touch, to drop a line, to have a cup of coffee with people she had met through business. Each week she made sure she networked with at least two people. No one who knew Hope ever wondered what she was up to. She make it part of her business to stay in touch. She turned that asset and all those cups of coffee, lunches and evening get-togethers into the start-up money for her new business.

Networking grows your business—and it *never* goes out of style. Whether you're introducing yourself and collecting business cards in a room full of other professionals or making friends on Facebook, networking connects you to your future: new people who have the power to hire you, purchase your products, connect you to other networks, bring you new opportunities or become golden referral sources.

LIVE NETWORKING EVENTS

Live networking events present a great place to start. They are low-cost and easy to execute. Whether you're at a Chamber of Commerce mixer, a professional organization meeting, or an event specifically designed for networking, new connections spell your success.

Amazingly, many people go to networking events and sit at the same table with the same people they already know. The most effective strategy in networking is to actually **network**. Imagine that. You are up and moving around, talking to as many people as you can, actually meeting some new folks.

Top 10 Tips for Live Networking Events

1. **Have a Goal.** Determine your goal for the event before you arrive. Who do you think will be there? How can you open the conversation? Give yourself a specific number of things to achieve. Write them down on a 3 x 5 card and slip it into your wallet or purse. Your goal might be to talk to 15 new people, collect 20 new cards or set five appointments. When you are clear about your intentions before you walk into the room, you'll achieve what you set out to accomplish.

2. **Approach Groups.** People often feel shy about approaching a group of people based on old fears of not fitting in, interrupting a group of friends or being rejected. What a big, fat trap this is. Silence that saboteur voice in your head. Instead remember that everyone at the networking event came for the same reason you did: to meet new people and, hopefully, some new prospects. If you are not a natural conversationalist, remember your written intentions, the fact everyone is there for the same reasons as you. Walk up, put out your hand and introduce yourself.

3. **Ask Questions First. Tell About You Later.** Engaging with others through fun and poignant questions always makes you welcome. One topic resonates with almost everyone you talk to—them. People love to be asked about themselves, their business, even why they are at the event. By asking about them first through polite, inquisitive questions, you accomplish two things. First, people will be put at ease by your genuine interest. They will feel comfortable sharing. Second, it gives you the opportunity to learn more about them so you can uncover more of their needs.

4. **Deliver Your Brief Elevated Speech.** Practice delivering your Elevated Speech before you go. Then you'll sound polished not tongue-tied when your moment comes to share. Keep it brief. What are you an expert in and what do you do for customers. "I'm an expert in making money. I show people how to make money in three days." Be brief, to the point and inspire your listener to ask for more.

5. **Be a Connector.** Want to be a hit with almost anyone? Ask for a description of their Ideal Prospect. Who are they looking for? Your commitment is that if you meet someone who fits their profile, you'll introduce them whether it's at this event or later. You become the connector. When you show the interest to ask how you can be of service in this way, you instantly become someone others want to talk to and be with.

6. **Take Notes.** Who remembers all those people they meet at an event? Not many can keep it all straight hours later. So when you meet someone, ask for her card and then write notes on the back as you talk. Do this even or perhaps especially when you've met her before. Write down interesting things about her,

about the kind of referrals she wants and any pertinent personal information to help jog your memory about her later. This is the big reason we never recommend anyone get shiny business cards.

7. **Follow Up.** If you said you'd call someone next Tuesday, make sure you follow through and do that. Read the notes on her card to remind you about your follow-up commitments. Send her a thank-you note for having a great conversation with you. If you get some note cards made with your photo on them, your new contact will remember you quickly. By following up, you monetize your networking efforts by creating a new source for referrals or maybe even a new prospect. This is why you went to the event in the first place.

8. **Put Them In Your Database.** You know all those cards you've collected? They do you no good cluttering your desk. Make sure that you get the contact information into your database and onto your Power 100 so that you can continue to build a relationship with each person. If you don't do this step, why did you take the time to go to the event? This is one of the pay-offs for your good work.

9. **Track Your Statistics.** Now track what happened so you know which events provide a great return. How many people did you meet? How many did you follow up with... everyone, right? How many follow-ups turned into a referral or new prospect for you? And lastly, how many new prospects turned into a customer? By tracking this information, you'll have a superior idea of what your marketing and sales efforts produce. You can make sound decisions when you are armed with the information that counts and all the mystery that seems to surround sales melts away.

10. **Have Fun and Make it a Game.** People at networking events are all in the same boat: wanting to connect, feeling awkward, learning to talk effectively about their business, and looking for connections. So remember to have fun with it, be light and make it into an exciting game.

SPEAK!

If you are comfortable on your feet, speaking in front of a live audience of Ideal Prospects delivers amazing returns. If you're not comfortable on your feet, get comfortable.

Speaking is powerful because your audience sees you in action. They have an opportunity to connect to you, be inspired by what you discuss and get motivated to put what you offer into their life. Speaking enables you to start to build trust, and without trust in our relationships with prospects, there is no sale. Just like Referrals, prospects who meet you at speaking events know something about you: they know an organization they trust, trusts you to speak. They begin their interactions with you at a deeper level.

Where I Can Speak

NAME OF GROUP	PHONE	WHAT YOU WANT THEM TO DO	WHEN YOU'LL CONTACT THEM

But there's a trick to speaking.

You are speaking to sell, not to educate.

Your job is not to completely sell them. If you sell too hard, they get zero out of your presentation. The trick is knowing how to sell *within* your presentation, without it feeling heavy-handed.

To do that, let's return to the work you did in Preeminence and Positioning, and get clear about how you want to talk to them about your business. You'll craft your topic around what we've discussed in so many places in this book: their problem or need. Your job is to create a little tension. What does the market place need now, what does this audience need?

YOUR JOB IS NOT TO COMPLETELY EDUCATE THEM. IF YOU DO, THEN THEY HAVE ALL THEY NEED TO SOLVE THEIR PROBLEM WITHOUT YOU— OR AT LEAST THEY THINK THEY DO.

Speaking, for our purposes, is a marketing and sales opportunity. If you treat a speaking event as an education opportunity, you're going to give the audience all the solutions they need. Your audience will stand up and applaud. They will walk to the back of the room and tell you how great your presentation was. They will be full of energy and smiles. Then they will walk away, happy and satisfied. But they will not be buyers.

You need to understand the mental condition of the people sitting in front of you. They come hungry for information, looking for ways to solve their problems or address their needs. They are already in a certain amount of tension because they need to do something. They just don't know what. You then hand them lots of good ideas. Tension relieved. They aren't hungry any more. They are full, and you filled them. There's no reason for them to buy anything from you because you fed them to full.

WHEN YOU SPEAK YOU NEED TO MAINTAIN OR EVEN INCREASE THEIR TENSION.

Tension puts every buyer into action. And you do that by focusing your presentation on their problem, not the solution. You do need to establish your credentials and show you have the chops to tackle their needs. That's where some of those Success Stories come in handy. Frame your presentation this way:

- Assure them you are going to share as much as you can in the time that you have.
- Present your credentials and why you're uniquely qualified to solve these problems and address those needs.
- Discuss the typical problems that the market is experiencing. Paint them a picture of what it looks and feels like. Draw them in with emotions. Make it resonate.
- Make your offer (more on this in a minute).
- Share some Success Stories of customers who have had those problems and the results they experienced in working with you.
- Ask them "What will happen if you don't address this problem or need?"
- Invite them to take your Top-of-Funnel offer.

The second big speaker no-no you've probably experienced yourself: the speaker holds their offer until the end of the presentation or phone call. The audience expects this and starts to disengage, getting themselves ready for what comes next. Too few people turn in their contact sheets or fill in your offer sheet. They've become distracted.

There's a brilliant way to beat this: plan to stop at the mid-point of your presentation and make your offer. Have all the paperwork on their tables before you start so you don't have the disturbance of passing out information. Tell them to fill in their contact sheet because you're going to pull one name for a special something—an iPOD, a free consultation with you, something of value. While they are filling in their paperwork, you can field a few questions and then make your offer. What do you want them to do? Offer no more than one option. Otherwise, you'll confuse them with choices. Get their contact sheets and pull the winner of the free offer. Then continue with your presentation, and make your offer again as you approach the end. Close your presentation a few minutes early or on time to show your respect. Then head to the back of the room with all or most of the contact sheets and make yourself available to those who want to buy from you.

New speakers also tend to cram too much into a presentation. Remember that if you're speaking the whole time, giving more and more information, you're increasing the risk that they won't be able to keep up; or worse, that they'll tune you out completely.

Remember to involve them in your talk by helping them to see the "gap" between where they are and where they want to be. Remind them about what they want to accomplish, the benefits of working with you. Speak to the gap and make it real for them. Then speak about your products or services as a way to bridge that gap.

You are giving them as many ideas as you have time for right now, and let them know exactly how they can get more. When they feel the gap, understand the value of closing it, and see an easy way to bridge that with your products and services, making a sale becomes much easier.

As you finish your presentation, make the next step with you very clear and very easy for them. Make sure your forms are simple and quick. You want to make it easy for them to say "Yes."

Now that you know the tricks, start keeping an eye out. You'll find speaking opportunities everywhere. Choose the places your Ideal Prospect frequents. To help a networking group decide to bring you in as a speaker, put together a packet of information including your photo, your business brochure, and a list of several speaking topics. If you've spoken in the past, list some of the places you've spoken. Most networking organizations feature keynote speakers as part of their events, so you can not only establish yourself as an expert, but get exposure to a whole room full of Ideal Prospects all at once. That's worth all the extra effort of speaking.

SOCIAL NETWORKING

Call it whatever you want—social networking is networking. You are just doing it on-line.

Everyone seems to be talking about the phenomenon of social networking (also called social media). With over 600,000 people joining Facebook every *day*, no business owner can afford to ignore the power of on-line networks as a way to generate new prospects and customers. The trick is to figure out how to get your social networking efforts to translate into real prospects instead of an enormous time drain. It's easy to lose hours and hours sifting through vacation pictures and posts about kid's dance recitals from old college buddies instead of developing new friends and then new prospects.

Yet the reason that social networking can be so effective in generating new business is because people love to do business with people they know.

Think about it. If you had two people vying for your business and they both had pretty much the same offer, and if you knew slightly more about one of them—maybe they grew up in the same town as you or they have kids the same age as yours or they really like strawberry smoothies for breakfast—you'd be much more likely to do business with the one you know, even if what you know about the person doesn't have anything to do with their product or service.

Lily was offering a class and having difficulty getting people to sign up. She turned to social networking, in particular Twitter and began offering really sound advice to the people who started to follow her. Soon there were over 1200 people following her. Now she had an audience, so she figured it was time to make a simple Top-of-Funnel offer to draw interested prospects from Twitter to her website. The offer was a free poster. Over they came, leaving Twitter to connect with her through her website. Now she had their contact information because they left their e-mail address to get the FREE poster. Lily's next job was to turn them from very distant relationships to warm "friends." She began to inform them about what she had to offer that would interest them: a class. Twelve people signed up! Why change something that works? So Lily used this approach several more times. Each time she successfully drew some of her Twitter crowd to her website with the the free offer and then some into a class. Not only is this a great example of how to use social networking, it's a pretty good Product Funnel, too. Lily used Twitter to change her business.

ONE TO FIVE RATIO

If you're using social networking with the goal of expanding your business, a key to success is to remember the "social" part of the equation.

If you relentlessly post about your products, services and business offerings—pounding them over and over with "buy, buy, buy"—you will turn people off or get the reputation of being a spammer. And that's the polite word. Our rule of thumb on postings-to-promotions is one business or promotional post for every four-to-five personal, non-business related or business-helpful posts (a quote, article, or video of interest, for example).

BEING SOCIAL MEANS SHARING USEFUL INFORMATION ABOUT YOURSELF, BEING AUTHENTIC, SHOWING INTEREST AND RECIPROCATING WITH OTHERS.

Our intention is not to teach you how to set up your social networking pages or push the buttons to make them work. You will find a plethora of information and tutorials about all that on-line.

Our intention is to help you generate more customers.

That means you need to know how to use social networking strategically to generate new friends and new prospects. While it may seem cool to have 3,000 friends on Facebook or 10,000 people following you on Twitter, translating those numbers into revenue is what really matters for your business. To do that, you must figure out a way to get the contacts out of your social media list—not simply following you on Facebook, Twitter or wherever—and onto your database. Your objective must be to get them to your website, phone, e-mail or store where they can opt into your database or meet you and drop into your Product Funnel.

THINK FRIENDLY PROSPECTS

In building your lists on social media sites, keep in mind that you're not just looking for "friends." You want friends who are also prospects. That means you want to connect with people in your target market; with people who can either hire you or connect you with those that would; and with potential partners and joint venture contacts. Now they might not show up as prospects, connectors or partners right away. Most often it takes a little time for things to evolve. But your patience is rewarded when you get what you're after: relationships that build your business.

The power in social networking comes from the exponential quality of the exposure. If you post content of value to others and they forward your post, then you not only reach your own list of people but their list as well. Instead of reaching 1,000 people on your list, for example, your post about "Five Ways to Increase Your Energy" would reach 6,000 when five people on your list forwarded it to their lists of 1,000 each. It's the new, new math. And don't forget to include the link to your website at the end of the post with an offer for a free report on "The Top 10 Super Foods for More Energy."

Listen closely as this is the true point of social networking for business: You want them to cross over from following you on Facebook, LinkedIn, Twitter or any other social networking page to following you via your website (or e-mail, phone or store) to grab your Top-of-Funnel offering.

Now you have them in your database! A friend becomes a prospect just like that.

WHICH SITES TO CHOOSE

With new social networking sites coming on line every day, how do you choose which ones to use? We recommend you start with the core group of Facebook, Twitter and LinkedIn. It's best to choose fewer sites and maintain consistent presence on them than to spread yourself too thin. If you have video or are committed to creating it, YouTube should be on your list. Again, go back to your target audience. Find and participate on the sites where you find your best prospects hanging out.

NOW GET OUT OF THE HOUSE

We've discussed just a very few of the many ways and places for you to network. Your opportunities, really, are limitless. You can network at PTA meetings, on the train commuting to your job, while working out at the gym—just about anywhere and anytime. Your job is to be ever-vigilant to the opportunities around you to connect and make new friends.

How you can network is equally diverse. We've discussed going to events, speaking and social networking to spark your creativity. But there are many more ways to network—podcasts, videocasts, blogs, articles on-line and off, and more.

Set a goal for yourself to get out and network at least once this week. Track what happens. Then got out next week and do it again. Make adjustments on what you learned the first week, the second week, the tenth week, and you'll get better and better with the rewards to show for it.

[summary]

- In today's market you need to make connections both off-line and on-line to find new prospects.
- Networking off-line and on-line enables you to do that.
- In-person networking events offer you great opportunities to meet your Ideal Prospect.
- When you show interest in the person in front of you and ask how you can help connect her to her Ideal Prospect, you will be remembered and assisted in return.
- Take notes as you talk to people, follow-up when you return home, add them to your database and track your results.
- Speaking engagements provide the opportunity to meet a room of Ideal Prospects all at once in a way that gives you credibility and trust fast.
- When speaking, your job is to create buyers, not satisfied listeners. Create some tension by focusing on their problem or need, as well as the results others have attained by working with you. Don't give away your solution.
- Make your offer at the mid-point of your talk, not at the end.
- Remember to keep it simple. Don't cram in too much information.
- Social networking is a must for every business if your Ideal Prospect is on-line.
- The key to successful social networking is to entice your reader to follow you to your website, phone, e-mail or store.
- Write, video, blog and speak from your spot of Preeminence and in a way that showcases your Positioning.

- Determine where to network based on where your Ideal Prospect is likely to be.
- To find new prospects you must get out of your house and network.

[exercises]

1. Where do your Ideal Prospects hang out? What events might they go to, what articles might they read, what blogs or social networking sites might they frequent?

———————————————————————————

———————————————————————————

———————————————————————————

2. From the list above, research and select three networking events to attend and put them on your calendar:

———————————————————————————

———————————————————————————

———————————————————————————

3. Based on your Preeminence and chosen Positioning, create three topics you can speak on with authority and authenticity.

———————————————————————————

———————————————————————————

———————————————————————————

4. Do you have Facebook, LinkedIn and Twitter accounts? If not, go set those up. If you have them but they are personal accounts for sharing with family and friends, create pages for your business. Invite people to follow your business.

5. Where else will you commit to networking off-line and on-line?

_____

_____

_____

Online Outreach
TOUCH YOUR PROSPECTS THROUGH THE WWW

Instant Global Access. *It used to be that if you wanted to reach thousands of people with your marketing message, you had to have big bucks to buy ads on television, radio, magazines or billboards. The Internet changed it all. The Web leveled the playing field. Not only did it give everyone access to the world, with the right strategy you can now reach your audience with very little expense. While there are all kinds of schemes and ways to spend big dollars using the Internet to market, it continues to be a low cost, highly effective way to connect with your potential customers when you have a plan before you spend even one dollar.*

YOUR WEBSITE

A website is definitely a requirement for businesses today, mandatory for almost everyone. Think of it this way. Twenty years ago if you had a business would you even think of not putting your phone number in the phone book?

THE INTERNET IS TODAY'S VERSION OF THE PHONE BOOK— AND NEWSPAPER, MAGAZINES, TV AND JUST ABOUT EVERY OTHER ADVERTISING SOURCE YOU CAN THINK OF.

No. Of course not. A business without a published phone number would have been dead.

Your site needs to be one of your most important customer "touch points," a specific moment when you connect with your prospect. Often it's the first touch point that the prospect has with you. It's the very beginning of the relationship. Do they feel engaged? Do they feel overwhelmed and confused? Can they easily find the information they're looking for?

Your website serves as a medium for you to connect in conversation with your customers. It's a place for you to share news and updates, educate and advise, get feedback and create community. It's a place for you to host on-line and virtual events: webinars, teleclasses, on-line seminars. It's how you begin to lead your prospects through at least the top of your Product Funnel. Drawing from the top of your Funnel, your site offers e-books, videos, podcasts, and how-to articles so your prospects can get to know you and develop trust in you. And of course, it's a place to sell products: everything from downloadable reports or e-books to merchandise or services purchased through your shopping cart.

We're going to share all the basics you need for on-line marketing here. We are interested in the strategy of building the right website, not the buttons that need to be pushed or the code that needs to be written. Never, ever let anyone build you a website or change the one you have without creating your website strategy first. Otherwise, you'll be blowing your money into the wind.

INTERNET MARKETING MAGIC

Internet marketing includes all the ways that we market products and services over the Internet. In a nutshell: You drive traffic to your site. The site captures visitors' names and contact information. Then you work these prospects through your Product Funnel and convert them into paying customers.

Simple.

Not so fast.

That's what it looks like from *your* side, from an operational point of view. But that's not the perspective that leads to success.

First we're going to lay out some of the basics you need to know about internet marketing. Then we're going to turn our attention to the most important viewpoint of your website: *how the visitor wants to interact with your site*. And it's not the same way you look at it.

INTERNET BASICS

Internet marketing is a beautiful thing. It works for you even while you're sleeping or vacationing. Your website is open for visitors and business even when you're out.

While this might seem basic, reviewing some of the Internet marketing tools that can make a difference in your business will give you a background to determine which will work best for you. There are many types of websites and Internet marketing tools that suit different needs. Here's an overview of the key Internet marketing tools and how you might use them in your business. We recommend implementing several so you test several methods to see which work best in attracting your Ideal Prospect.

- **Website**: this is your primary on-line site. It presents the key information your visitor needs—the problem you address, services you offer, a bit about you and an offer that encourages them to call you or leave their e-mail address in exchange for the offer.

- **Landing Pages**: Also called a "squeeze" or "splash" page, this is a single page website where prospects "land" as a result of a specific campaign or ad prompt. It asks them to do one thing, such as buy a CD or download a report. It does not navigate back to your site or offer any other distractions.

- **Written Content**: Your written content on your website—articles, public relations, e-books and such—establishes your expertise and your Preeminence as well as communicating your key branding messages.

- **Video**: The fastest growing new communication tool, video will soon dominate the web. Video is the preferred method for learning and getting information these days because it's easy—it doesn't require us to click or read anything. YouTube is already the second most popular site (after Google).

- **Podcasts**: Audio broadcasts that can be downloaded to an IPod or MP3 player. Podcasts are very easy way to get content that you can listen to at your convenience. People can download the audio and listen anywhere they want.

- **Blog**: A "log" or diary-type entry about a topic you write about frequently and post for others to read and comment on.

- **Banner Ads**: Ads that you purchase and place on other sites that direct prospects to a specific product or service.

- **Affiliate Programs**: A program that gives others a reward for bringing you business or selling your products or services. Having an Affiliate Program allows you to expand your sales force and create other ambassadors for your business. You can also generate additional revenue by becoming an affiliate of other businesses and sharing that information with your database.

- **Pay-Per-Click Marketing**: These are the ads that pop up on the right-hand side of the screen when you do a search on Google or any other search engine. Those ads are limited to just a few words, so every word counts. There's an art and a science to writing these ads which take into consideration keyword searches. It's best to test a variety of phrases to see which pulls the best response.

- **Search Engine Optimization**: This refers to improving the natural or "organic" ranking that a site receives, whether it shows up on the first or the tenth page of a keyword search. You can optimize your ranking through tagging certain words in the code written for the site, linking and other methods. Good search engine professionals can also help you get ranked higher by evaluating your site, examining competitive sites, and editing yours. Changes take some time to register and optimization fluctuates frequently without guarantees.

- **E-mail Marketing**: Social media, texting, Instant Messaging and new communication innovations grab more of our attention every day but the e-mail in-box is still the center of many people's universe. Having a strong e-mail database is central to the success of your business. When used correctly, it can be a highly effective way to get information about your expertise, products and services in front of your prospects. Be very careful about SPAM.

The bottom line is this: if someone hasn't given you permission to e-mail them, then you are spamming. Furthermore, we live in an "unsubscribe" world. Good e-mail marketing *always* includes a way to unsubscribe, which means your prospect always has the option to break up with you... quickly and easily.

- **Auto-responder**: Programs that allow you to automate the follow-up messages and flow of content to your e-mail database. Multiple messages can be put into an auto-responder series so you can stay in front of your prospect. Just because they said, "no" to your offer one day doesn't mean that they never want to buy.

Unless you have a strong background in technology or Internet marketing, we highly recommend leaving the creation of this Activator to a professional website designer or Internet marketing expert.

This is a good place to pull in team members to help you.

As the business owner you lead the team and hold the vision for your company. You don't have to do everything on your own.

YOU'VE GOT EXACTLY *SEVEN SECONDS* TO GRAB THE ATTENTION OF A VISITOR TO YOUR WEBSITE, OR THEY'RE OFF TO SOMETHING ELSE. SEVEN SECONDS...

But before you start a new website or change your existing one, before you spend one, single dime, there is something you need to do—have a strategy for your website.

CREATE THE "RIGHT" SITE

More and more prospects use the Internet to find and evaluate businesses they want to work with or buy from. Your website will most likely be the number one way your prospects will find you.

This is the reason we want you to start with a little strategy before spending any of your time and money building the site.

You need to address three questions that will enable you to build a successful website:

- What is the purpose of your site? Is it to prove your credentials, support you non-Internet business, build your customer database, or to sell products and services? Maybe a bit of all four?

- How will people find you? You must consider the question before you begin as it will affect how your site is designed. Having a great site is important, but getting traffic to come to and stay on your website is equally critical.

- What do you want them to do when they come to your site? *This is the biggest, most important question of the three.* If you don't know what you want them to do, they won't either. When you know—and it's usually one thing not several—then your website will be designed to showcase that One Thing so they find it and see it quickly. Seven seconds, remember. Tick.Tick.Tick.

The home page is paramount. It's the page that gets them excited, interested to explore more, and take action. Around 65 percent of visitors view only 1.63 pages! That's not much. The better the home page the more likely they are to look around, visit multiple pages on your site and follow your Call To Action (what you want them to do).

They are coming to your website to figure out what you offer and how they can benefit from it. The first thing they need to see on your home page is *what's in it for them*. What's the problem that they have? Show them you understand their situation. Tell them what you offer and how it will benefit them.

WRITE YOUR HOME PAGE COPY ABOUT THEM, NOT YOU.

Only when they've read enough to understand what's in it for them will they then begin to explore the rest of your site.

Next we want you to think about what you have to offer—to create what we call the "bright, shiny, red car" of your business. Your website home page should look just like the showroom. You need to identify what your bright, shiny, red sports car is and place it prominently on your home page.

Did you know that your website home page has prime real estate? Location, location, location applies on your website, too. Where exactly is the prime real estate on the home page? Specialists have determined that there is a predictable pattern to how our eyes travel over a website.

The prime real estate is the top left-hand corner. That's where the visitor's eye goes first. Almost always that's reserved for your company name and logo. Then the eye sweeps down and to the right. The next prime piece of website real estate can be found on the right about a quarter or a third of the way from the top of the page. That's a great place to put your shiny car or special offer or Call To Action. What will you place in your prime real estate? Whatever you want them to do when they come to your site.

You need to determine your website strategy so your site is built from Day One with the answer to those three questions in mind. And remember—seven seconds. That's all the time you have to grab their attention. So eliminate anything that isn't necessary. Put on your best New Yorker and get right to the point. No "Welcome" mat message. No long front page copy about you. No blah, blah, blah. Get straight to their problem and what's in it for them.

Pass the seven-second test and watch your website visitors engage.

There is so much more to Internet Marketing, and the tools available to you change so fast. This is a great area to get help from expert team members who know how to get results—and we'd love to be the ones who help you. Get the ball rolling for your website by connecting with us via the Resources page at the end of the book.

[summary]

- The Internet is magic because it keeps your website open and available for your Ideal Prospect to visit any time, from anywhere.
- There are a variety of website types and Internet marketing tools for you to use to bring Ideal Prospects to your door.
- On average you have seven seconds to engage your website visitor or they are gone.
- Before you spend one more dime on a website—a new one or your existing site—determine what your website strategy is.

- Three critical questions to answer before you make any changes to your site are: What is the purpose of your site? How will people find your site? What do you want them to do when they get there (one thing only)?
- Write home page copy that speaks to your Ideal Prospect's problem or need. Share what you can do to solve that problem. The copy isn't about you!
- Place your Call To Action in a high visibility place on your site. No clicking or scrolling to find it.
- Use the high-visibility places on your home page to best advantage. This is where your What You Want Them To Do goes.
- Be direct and to the point in your copy and everything about your site. Use your seven seconds wisely.

[exercises]

1. If you presently have a website, what do you want people to do when they come to your site?

_____

_____

_____

2. Is what you want them to do obvious, or do they need to hunt, click or scroll to find where you've hidden it? If it's hidden, how can you "unhide" it on the home page?

_____

_____

_____

3. How do people find your website today?

_____

_____

_____

4. Which Internet tools are appropriate for your Ideal Prospect? How can these tools draw more of them to your site?

_____

_____

_____

5. Do you have Google Analytics running on your website? If not, call your website developer and get it now. It's free. When you do, answer these questions:

a. How many discrete visitors came to your site last month? _____

_____

b. How many pages did they view? _____

_____

c. How long did they stay? _____

_____

d. How many opted-in for your free offer? _____

_____

PART THREE

Expansion

Now that you've established a strong Foundation and put in place all the Customer Activation methods appropriate for your Ideal Prospect, your business processes need to be just as strong.

Good systems are required to support your continued expansion. The final part of your Customer Generator System includes a brief look at the support systems required to keep your business flourishing.

Then we pull it altogether with your Mini Marketing Plan: your blueprint for more customers, more money and a better system.

Support Systems
HEALTHY BUSINESS AND HEALTHY FINANCES

Your Back Office. *Your support systems include all the tools that keep your business running smoothly and efficiently. With all the energy you've invested in establishing a solid Foundation and generating a flood of new customers through the Customer Activators, you don't want to get derailed by overlooking some financial or business detail. Strong systems support your growth. You stay focused on building your business rather than rebuilding or repairing it.*

S upport systems are essential, and there's a time and a place to bring them in.

If you are not out marketing and selling, you don't have many financials to worry about or customers to service.

Conversely, you don't want to be so focused on making money and closing deals that you neglect the structures that support you. So take an honest look at where you are in your business. When you are making money or more money, bring in the systems.

SOME BUSINESS OWNERS SPEND TOO MUCH OF THEIR VALUABLE TIME "GETTING READY" BY OVERINVESTING IN SYSTEMS INSTEAD OF GETTING OUT AND TALKING TO CUSTOMERS.

E-MAIL DATABASE MANAGEMENT SYSTEM

A strong e-mail database is a key ingredient in your marketing arsenal. It captures valuable information about your customers, such as their contact information, preferences and patterns. It tracks each "touch point" you have with them and can automatically send messages and content at each step of the sales cycle. It reports all this in detail so you can see what's really going on with your prospects and customers.

If you have a Free Offer on your website, you need an e-mail database system. Otherwise, where do all those names and e-mail addresses go? And when you come back from a networking event, you need to put the business card info that you've gathered someplace other than the top of your desk.

That means an e-mail database is probably one of the first systems you'll need.

The good news is they come in all shapes, sizes, functionalities and price. There's a good, affordable one for every business. And as you investigate, make sure there's enough room for the growth you expect now and for the next several years.

Which is the right e-mail system for you? That depends a lot on what you need to track to grow your particular kind of business and the size of the database you currently have. You want a system that can support you now and grow with you as you achieve more of your revenue goals.

- For smaller companies or start-ups with databases of less than 10,000, we recommend I-Contact. We like their functionality, price and flexibility. And it's easy to use.

- For larger companies with databases exceeding 10,000, check out awebber, salesforce or Infusionsoft.

Do your research and get clear about the functionality your business needs. All good e-mail database management systems are transferable and upgradable as you add more contacts. Basically, as long as you can export your contacts into an Excel spreadsheet, you can move them between programs as your needs change or you outgrow your choice.

YOUR BANK. YOUR PARTNER

Check with your local county about business licensing requirements and file your DBA (Doing Business As) documents. You will need these to open a business account. Open a separate checking account for your business and keep it separate from your personal account. Talk to several banks to understand how they work and treat business customers. FROM THE VERY FIRST DAY, YOU MUST SEPARATE YOUR BUSINESS FINANCES FROM YOUR PERSONAL FINANCES.

You'll be surprised how different it is from personal accounts. Choose a bank that has a good track record of working with small businesses. Do your research and ask questions.

If you're looking to get a loan, remember that the best time to ask for money is when you have money. Better to ask when the business is growing and you already have some capital than waiting until desperate times call for desperate measures. Telegraphing that kind of urgency to a banker doesn't set you up for success. It's a good idea to develop a relationship with your banker ahead of time as well so that you don't just show up at their desk when you want something from them. Keep in mind that banks are only one option for funding your growth. These days you'll also find a number of private lenders looking for some great businesses to fund. Look around, ask around and you'll find numerous options for your review.

And, by the way, while you're at your business bank, get a business credit card also. That's the other way you should be separating your personal life from your business life. Every time you buy something ask yourself "Is this a personal expense or a business expense?" Then use the right credit card.

A GOOD CPA

Another key player on your team is a CPA or accountant who specializes in working with small business owners. Ask peers and colleagues for referrals. Tell them you want someone who can create tax strategies, not just tax compliance.

Those two talents are not always found in one CPA.

As a small business owner, you'll likely utilize many contractors as you grow your business. When you pay people as a contractor it means they

YOU WANT A CPA WHO IS GREAT NOT ONLY AT TAX COMPLIANCE; YOU WANT ONE WHO IS STELLAR AT TAX STRATEGIES.

are not your employees. They have other customers they work for besides you. If they're only working for you now, then you should be paying them as employees, which likely means paying their taxes. A great CPA will guide you through this "contractor vs. employee" discussion to help you determine what is best now for your business.

Everything you spend on your business could also be a write-off on your taxes. A CPA who knows how to balance impeccable compliance with business strategies such as write-offs will support you with ways to minimize your tax burden and pay what you owe.

ENTITY OR NOT

There will be a point in time in your business when you are making some serious change. As you work with more customers and have more contractors and employees on your payroll, your liability increases. Now is the time to consider incorporating your business.

Incorporating provides you with certain protections, privileges and obligations. You are personally protected from law suits and claims that could attach your personal assets. You receive tax privileges only afforded to incorporated businesses. You are obligated to report certain information to your local, state and federal governments at periodic intervals.

How do you know when your business should incorporate? There is no hard and fast rule. We recommend you work with a company that specializes in advising you on the best entity choice for your company, and then has the ability to do the incorporation paperwork for you. You can do it yourself, and it will certainly cost less. But do you know enough to choose the right entity and is that where you want to spend your time, money and effort?

If you aren't convinced an entity is really needed, please reflect on this. There are two tax codes in effect today: one for individuals and one for businesses. Which one do you think is more advantageous?

MAKE IT EASY TO GIVE YOU MONEY

When you market and sell on-line, you must be able to accept and receive credit card payments. Every step of the way, every engagement an Ideal Prospect or customer has with you needs to be easy. That includes buying from you. Credit cards are easy. Just how often do you use cash these days? Probably very little for on-line transactions, purchases from companies you haven't done business with before, or bigger ticket buys.

If you're just starting out, you can use a third-party on-line processing service such as PayPal or Google Check Out to receive payments. This requires customers to establish an account. PayPal or Google Check Out verify the financial information, receive the payment and then transfer it to your stated bank, less their transaction fee.

To be able to accept credit directly through your website or directly into your account without PayPal or Google in the middle, you have to establish a merchant account, a bank account specifically designed to receive credit card transactions. Talk to your business bank about their merchant services, look at places like Costco and Sam's Club as they offer merchant services. There are fees for moving that credit card transaction from your customer's bank to yours. So check out the fees in addition to the other services merchant account businesses offer.

Then you want to work with your web designer and technology team to create a "shopping cart" on your website. You'll need shopping cart functionality on your site to process payments. That capability might be in the e-mail database management system you are investigating. If not, start your investigation with services like 1ShoppingCart.

TRACK YOUR FINANCES

Whether you hire a bookkeeper or do it yourself, all healthy businesses require up-to-the minute visibility into their financial status. On-line accounting software systems like QuickBooks make it easy to keep track of your money, profits and losses, forecasts, and budgets. These applications will save time and alleviate a great deal of stress so you can focus on doing what you do best.

If your business is established and you're making money right now, it's convenient to have a database system that integrates with QuickBooks. That enables a transaction to go from your shopping cart, through your merchant account, to your bank, into your database and into QuickBooks in what will feel like one step. Your CPA, bookkeeper—or you—will not have to pull your records and enter that information manually into QuickBooks.

ASSESS WHAT YOU NEED

Take a moment right now to look at the support systems you currently have in your business. Are you adequately supported? What's missing? What would make your business run more smoothly? What can be automated? Healthy support systems act like the "wind beneath the wings" of your business. What must you have in place to allow you to soar?

[summary]

- Good, healthy businesses add systems just before they need them.
- An e-mail database management system might be your first investment as it stores all the visitors who opt-in on your website and enables you to legally communicate with them.
- Separate your personal banking accounts and expenses from your business bank and expenses.
- Shop for your business bank. It might not be where you do your personal banking , as terms and conditions are different for business accounts. Look around. Don't just choose what you know.
- A good CPA, accountant or bookkeeper is an asset to your business. You want a CPA who is a great tax strategist, not just wonderful at tax compliance.
- Based on the taxes you want to save, the liability you want to avoid and the Government obligations you are willing to meet,

turning your business into a legal corporation is an important step for your business to consider.

• Talk to entity experts before you incorporate to get the advice you need to choose the entity type that is best for your business needs.

• Make it easy for customers to buy from you. Taking credit cards is almost mandatory for any business. You can use PayPal or Google Check Out if you are just getting started. If your business is making money, consider getting a merchant account from your bank.

• Make sure you can process payments and flow transaction information into your database management system via "shopping cart" functionality. Have your website developer connect what you sell on your website to your functioning shopping cart so you can sell on the internet.

• Track your revenue and expenses using an accounting system like QuickBooks. Many database management systems have applications that integrate with QuickBooks, so that transaction information can flow automatically from your shopping cart to your bank account to your accounting records.

[exercises]

1. Is it time for you to consider an e-mail database management system or upgrade the one you have? Which ones will you investigate and by when?

_____

_____

_____

2. Check into the business accounts and services offered by three banks. Determine which best meets your needs.

   _____

   _____

   _____

3. Is your current CPA or accountant strategically savvy about business taxation? If your CPA is great at compliance only, it's time to investigate a new team member for your business. What questions will you ask candidates when you call?

   a. Do you routinely work with small businesses, LLCs and S Corporations?

      _____

      _____

      _____

   b. What are some new tax strategies you believe every business should consider or use?

      _____

      _____

      _____

   c. Other questions? _____

      _____

      _____

      _____

4. Are you ready for an entity?

   a. Are you making good money in your business? _____

      _____

      _____

      _____

b. Do you need to be concerned about liability with employees or contractors? _____

_____

_____

_____

c. Can new tax strategies save you money? _____

_____

_____

_____

d. Call three entity companies to determine which entity type is best for you and which entity company should be your new Team member.

_____

_____

_____

5. Call around to see who's offering a great merchant account program if you need more than PayPal or Google Check Out.

_____

_____

_____

6. Do you have an accounting system? QuickBooks (not Quicken). Talk to your CPA and go get it... now.

_____

_____

_____

Your Mini Marketing Plan

PUT YOUR CUSTOMER GENERATOR SYSTEM TOGETHER

Ready, Go! *You've learned about the Foundational pieces of your business: Preeminence, Positioning, Product Funnel, Revenue Model and Your Extraordinary Offer.*

Y ou've explored the Activation steps to take that will guarantee you a flood of new customers: The Power 100, Power Hour, Referral System, Reviving the Dead, Partnering, Networking, and Online Outreach.

You've also taken a look at Expansion via the support systems you'll put in place to sustain the growth of your business. Now it's time to pull it altogether into your action plan.

Strategy is great and it's important as your first step, but you just have ideas until you put the strategies into action.

Obviously you cannot tackle all these brilliant ideas at once. As you've read, some things have excited you more than others. Some things will appeal to your Ideal Prospect faster than others. Choosing a few—not everything—is an important step now. Tackling too many at once means you succeed at none, and that makes you feel defeated, frustrated and insecure.

But we know that won't happen because you are something else—You Are a Leader. A Leader of your Ideal Prospects. A Leader of your Customers. A Leader of your Team. A Leader of Yourself. It's up to you to stand in your power, share your expertise, draw on your confidence and lead your customers where they want to go. Your customers depend on you for that.

A FABULOUS FOUR

Here's your mini-marketing plan. Right now, choose two Foundation steps and two Activation steps. Choose only two from those sections if you are just starting your business, regrouping or making just a bit of money. Four gives you very specific areas to focus on, and not get overwhelmed. That will generate your momentum. That will bring you success.

Once you have these four humming, then you will free up more resources and energy to work on the next set you want to implement. Trying to take on more will actually sabotage your efforts so stay focused.

The Exercises we've included at the end of each chapter create a Mini Marketing Plan template for you to fill in. We've also included some tactical ideas under each of the system steps to help you translate them into bite-sized tasks that you can start working on **today**.

COMFORT OR GROWTH?

As you select the four areas to work on, stay clear about the four that you *know* will have the biggest positive impact on your business. You're here because you want more customers.

Which of the steps will bring more customers to you fast?

Your answer might not look like the steps to which you feel most attracted. We tend to gravitate toward areas where we feel comfortable, but does that really best serve your business right now? Do they best serve your Ideal Prospect and current customers?

After you choose the steps that are best for your business, you want to tie each step to a business objective. How will each one specifically meet one of your goals? Then list:

- The tactical actions required,
- Who will be responsible for them and
- When it will be done.

This is everything you need to include to have a solid, clear plan. A solid, clear plan makes it easy for you to implement and adjust as you learn more about your Ideal Prospects and what they want. A solid, clear plan makes it so much easier for your employees and contractors to understand where you want to go, how you want to get there and their role in the journey.

Get Used To Success

IS IT OKAY WITH YOU IF LIFE GOT EASIER?

The Road Less Traveled. *You wouldn't have decided to start your own business if you weren't someone who loves challenge and likes to lead others. You were born to be an entrepreneur and be your own boss. Sometimes the stress of having your own business, generating customers and managing cash flow can cloud your vision. Maybe you even lose sight of your dream. Maybe you start telling yourself that it's just too hard or you don't have what it takes.*

When you start fantasizing about getting a W2 job, you know it's time for a good whack on the head. We know because we've been there.

That's why we all need team and a good system to keep us on track. We know that the Customer Generator System works. We use it ourselves, and we've coached hundreds of business owners just like you to success beyond their dreams. You can stop struggling and free yourself from the mire of confusion by following this system. You can finally have a steady stream of eager new customers instead of panicking about just breaking even. It doesn't mean that as a business owner you won't have new challenges and frustrations. That's life.

But would it be OK with you to trade in your current stresses for some new ones? Instead of going around and around worrying about how to get more customers, how about fretting about where to invest all your new cash flow?

YOU GOTTA HAVE TEAM

One thing we know for sure, this is not a time to go it alone.

The most successful business owners we see are those who continually learn, network, ask questions and get coaching support. They place themselves in groups where they can leverage the power of synergy and keep themselves accountable.

now what?

For many of you, you now have everything in your hands to turn your business on its proverbial ear.

For others *Customers Are The Answer to Everything* has opened your eyes to how to start. Perhaps a little extra, personal guidance is what it takes to fine-tune the business jumpstart you want to achieve.

We want to extend to you our own Extraordinary Offer--to personally get you on your way to all the customers you want through a free Marketing GAP Analysis session. These 30-minute sessions will give you one-on-one time with a Marketing Strategist trained by Martha and Chris...or perhaps with Martha and Chris themselves. Each Marketing Strategist is skilled in rapidly determining where you are versus where you want to be, plus the next steps to get you moving in the direction of your customers.

YOUR NEXT STEP:

✓ **Call to schedule your FREE 30-minute GAP Analysis session 1-530-878-1491.**

177

Wide Awake Marketing customizes all of its coaching, products and services to perfectly fit you. During your 30-minute GAP Analysis we're working with you to determine your next steps, not fitting you into some pre-determined cookie-cutter approach. And we'll discuss how we can work together to plan and execute your marketing next-steps by identifying and attracting your customers through such services as:

- Virtual 8-Week "Get Customers" Workshop

- Private Marketing Coaching

- Marketing Strategy Services
    - Branding
    - Positioning
    - Marketing Plans
    - Website Strategy

- Marketing Implementation Services
    - Website creation
    - Website marketing copywriting
    - Copywriting
    - Search Engine Optimization (SEO)
    - Keyword analysis
    - Logo creation

Candidly, most books don't call for action. This one demands it. Many of you have read the entire book first without completing any of the written forms. That's fine because you don't have to do this all by yourself. If you are one of those individuals—and we do hope you are— who is willing to stop in their tracks, turn in a new direction and start attracting customers the way they want to be attracted, then we will work together in some way.

We know it's difficult to see your business as others see it. We bring "new eyes". It's difficult to break old habits or the way you were trained. We bring "new ways." And frankly, customers change all the time—they are people after all, and we people are changing daily. That makes it hard to find the "new new" thing that's not the latest flashy trend and has staying power. We bring the "staying power."

SUCCESS STORY

Viventé is a successful organizational development and executive coaching business based in Australia (www.vivente.com.au). Yet their clients did not recognize that a company called Viventé existed. It was the Peter-or-Marg Show. Their clients recognized only the principals. They saw no company around them. Peter and Marg were at a crossroad. They wanted their business to grow yet it couldn't be solely dependent on them. How could they grow the business but not personally work all hours of the day? How could they step into a senior strategy and management role if they could not extricate themselves from the day-to-day? How could they continue to attract highly talented team and engage meaningfully with the client? And how the heck could they take a vacation, enjoy their family and have a personal life occasionally?

Their goal—move Viventé front and center as their brand.

During our GAP Assessment meeting, Wide Awake Marketing, together with Peter and Marg, determined their first actions—establish the Positioning on which to build the Viventé brand. Through interviews with them and, most importantly, a number of clients we determined what made them usefully and compelling different. Viventé develops high performance leadership to advance a high performance culture within their client's organization. When tested with their clients and prospects, this resonated perfectly.

With the key to creating Brand Viventé in hand, the next steps were to put it in play in public ways. A new website was mandatory as most corporations will investigate your website prior to returning your first call, responding to an email or accepting a meeting. The website would be a major contributor to demonstrating Brand Viventé. To support this on-line brand presence we chose blogging and search engine optimization as the first Internet Marketing leverages to be executed. Viventé began blogging, choosing a topic that demonstrates their "secret sauce" and speaks to a key corporate concern. Search engine optimization, executed to bring the right prospect not simply "get them on the first page of Google," will enable the *right* prospects to find them faster.

The results? First, the brand of Viventé is firmly planted in the minds of the principals, Peter and Marg. Now their clients understand they represent something bigger than just themselves, and for the team there are brand guidelines to enable them to stay true to what Brand Viventé stands for. It's critical to have the team on board as they get a chance to reinforce or undo the brand every day as they talk with clients and prospects. They now have a Thought Leadership platform from which they can create interesting and timely speaking topics. The blog is picking up readership, and most importantly, new prospects are contacting them.

Do they have more work to do to build Brand Viventé? You bet. Yet they can see they are on their way to their goal. Today Viventé has created a strong foundation and applied key activation leverages to attract their Ideal Prospect.

INVESTMENT OR EXPENSE?

The next choice is yours. Was this book a business expense—a nice read that you do nothing about—or is it a marketing investment because you put these steps into action?

This book was intended to be more than just ink on paper. Our goal is to open your eyes to what your customers really want and how you can give them precisely what they really want. If your eyes are open, your mind is curious, and your imagination stimulated, then commit to follow through.

We're going to tell you right now that you need to take action. Reading is nice. Doing something is superior and takes you really where you want to go, doesn't it? One step, then another, then the next. Pretty soon you're in big-time motion.

Read the book again, and this time do the exercises, write your notes and put pen to paper to make this information your knowledge. And call us to take your results above and beyond.

epilogue

We hope you have gained useful and valuable insights into your Ideal Prospect and how to bring them into your business joyfully. Now you know marketing isn't about you. It's about them—your Ideal Prospect, your Customers, your Clients. We hope we've also been able to share our enthusiasm for entrepreneurs and small business owners.

We are just like you. What's contained in this book is what we wish people had told us (if they even knew) when we were getting our MBA, working for big companies and out working on our own. But people didn't tell us. We suspect because they didn't know. Now you do. Go put it to good use.

Go forth and do great things.

Martha Hanlon
Chris Williams

about the authors

MARTHA HANLON

Martha is a thought-provoking marketing expert who spots trends and breaks a lot of marketing "rules" to deliver new results. Her forward-thinking has led to the identification of nine marketing leverages that create the fastest path to customers. Fun, engaging and a bit irreverent, Martha is passionate about the need for businesses to start talking to people in lively, authentic conversations—and to tell stories that help the world understand why they are important.

Martha has founded three marketing companies, after years leading product management and marketing divisions in Corporate America and worked with more than 500 companies from Fortune 100 to VC-backed start-ups to the auto dealer down the street to build brands, create new services and generate lead flow.

Martha has an MBA from The Wharton School, University of Pennsylvania and a B.S. from Duquesne University. She is a sought after writer, speaker and trainer. She is the primary author of money-Making Marketing. She currently sits on several Boards.

CHRIS WILLIAMS

Recognized by *Sacramento Magazine* as one of the top five sales experts in the California capitol area, Chris is a dynamic business builder, sought-after speaker and results-producing business coach. After training over 1,000 Xerox sales reps, she single-handedly built a $4 million per year Xerox distributorship of 13 sales people that grew 18 percent year over year. She blends her years of corporate experience with her hands-on entrepreneurial knowledge as a highly successful business owner into interactive, high-energy and high-content programs. Program participants report results like, "I increased my sales by 233 percent." "I closed 60 leads in 45 days." "I tripled my business in 90 days."

resources

We could put all the worksheets right here in the book for you to tear out, but who wants to work on 6" x 9" pieces of papers! So we've placed everything on a hidden page on our website available to all of our readers. You can pick up all the worksheets and resources in this book for free at www.WideAwakeMarketing.com/Resources.

And remember our invitation to you. Call us for a Marketing GAP Analysis. It's free and you'll spend 30 minutes with a marketing professional determining where you are, where you want to go and the next steps to get you there. Call 530-878-1491 to set up your appointment.

BUY A SHARE OF THE FUTURE IN YOUR COMMUNITY

These certificates make great holiday, graduation and birthday gifts that can be personalized with the recipient's name. The cost of one S.H.A.R.E. or one square foot is $54.17. The personalized certificate is suitable for framing and will state the number of shares purchased and the amount of each share, as well as the recipient's name. The home that you participate in "building" will last for many years and will continue to grow in value.

Here is a sample SHARE certificate:

YES, I WOULD LIKE TO HELP!

I support the work that Habitat for Humanity does and I want to be part of the excitement! As a donor, I will receive periodic updates on your construction activities but, more importantly, I know my gift will help a family in our community realize the dream of homeownership. **I would like to SHARE in your efforts against substandard housing in my community!** *(Please print below)*

PLEASE SEND ME _____ SHARES at $54.17 EACH = $ $_____

In Honor Of: _____

Occasion: (Circle One)   HOLIDAY   BIRTHDAY   ANNIVERSARY

     OTHER: _____

Address of Recipient: _____

Gift From: _____ *Donor Address:* _____

Donor Email: _____

I AM ENCLOSING A CHECK FOR $ $_____ PAYABLE TO HABITAT FOR HUMANITY OR PLEASE CHARGE MY VISA OR MASTERCARD *(CIRCLE ONE)*

Card Number _____ Expiration Date: _____

Name as it appears on Credit Card _____ Charge Amount $ _____

Signature _____

Billing Address _____

Telephone # Day _____ Eve _____

PLEASE NOTE: Your contribution is tax-deductible to the fullest extent allowed by law.
Habitat for Humanity • P.O. Box 1443 • Newport News, VA 23601 • 757-596-5553
www.HelpHabitatforHumanity.org

CPSIA information can be obtained at www.ICGtesting.com
Printed in the USA
BVOW060003040412

286810BV00002B/10/P